Pioneers

Other books in the History Firsthand series:

Pioneers

Mark McKain, *Book Editor*

Daniel Leone, *President*
Bonnie Szumski, *Publisher*
Scott Barbour, *Managing Editor*
David M. Haugen, *Series Editor*

GREENHAVEN
PRESS®

THOMSON
━━━━━★━━━━━ ™
GALE

San Diego • Detroit • New York • San Francisco • Cleveland
New Haven, Conn. • Waterville, Maine • London • Munich

LIBRARY OF CONGRESS CATALOGING-IN-PUBLICATION DATA

Pioneers / by Mark McKain, book editor.
   p. cm. — (History firsthand)
Includes bibliographical references and index.
ISBN 0-7377-1078-0 (alk. paper) —
ISBN 0-7377-1077-2 (pbk. : alk. paper)
   1. Pioneers—West (U.S.)—History—19th century—Juvenile literature.
2. Pioneers—West (U.S.)—Biography—Juvenile literature. 3. Frontier and pioneer life—West (U.S.)—Juvenile literature. 4. West (U.S.)—History—Juvenile literature.
[1. Pioneers—West (U.S.) 2. Frontier and pioneer life—West (U.S.) 3. West (U.S.)—History—19th century.] I. McKain, Mark. II. Series.

F596 .P55   2003
978'.02—dc21
                                                  2002000381

Contents

Reno, Nevada. Beckwourth also guided the first
wagon train of settlers through the pass.

Chapter 2: Preparing for the Journey West

Chapter 3: The Journey

Chapter 4: Encountering Native Americans

Chapter 5: Homesteading

Foreword

In his preface to a book on the events leading to the Civil War, Stephen B. Oates, the historian and biographer of Abraham Lincoln, John Brown, and other noteworthy American historical figures, explained the difficulty of writing history in the traditional third-person voice of the biographer and historian. "The trouble, I realized, was the detached third-person voice," wrote Oates. "It seemed to wring all the life out of my characters and the antebellum era." Indeed, how can a historian, even one as prominent as Oates, compete with the eloquent voices of Daniel Webster, Abraham Lincoln, Harriet Beecher Stowe, Frederick Douglass, and Robert E. Lee?

Oates's comment notwithstanding, every student of history, professional and amateur alike, can name a score of excellent accounts written in the traditional third-person voice of the historian that bring to life an event or an era and the people who lived through it. In *Battle Cry of Freedom*, James M. McPherson vividly re-creates the American Civil War. Barbara Tuchman's *The Guns of August* captures in sharp detail the tensions in Europe that led to the outbreak of World War I. Taylor Branch's *Parting the Waters* provides a detailed and dramatic account of the American Civil Rights Movement. The study of history would be impossible without such guiding texts.

Nonetheless, Oates's comment makes a compelling point. Often the most convincing tellers of history are those who lived through the event, the eyewitnesses who recorded their firsthand experiences in autobiographies, speeches, memoirs, journals, and letters. The Greenhaven Press History Firsthand series presents history through the words of first-person narrators. Each text in this series captures a significant historical era or event—the American Civil War, the

Great Depression, the Holocaust, the Roaring Twenties, the 1960s, the Vietnam War. Readers will investigate these historical eras and events by examining primary-source documents, authored by chroniclers both famous and little known. The texts in the History Firsthand series comprise the celebrated and familiar words of the presidents, generals, and famous men and women of letters who recorded their impressions for posterity, as well as the statements of the ordinary people who struggled to understand the storm of events around them—the foot soldiers who fought the great battles and their loved ones back home, the men and women who waited on the breadlines, the college students who marched in protest.

The texts in this series are particularly suited to students beginning serious historical study. By examining these first-hand documents, novice historians can begin to form their own insights and conclusions about the historical era or event under investigation. To aid the student in that process, the texts in the History Firsthand series include introductions that provide an overview of the era or event, timelines, and bibliographies that point the serious student toward key historical works for further study.

The study of history commences with an examination of words—the testimony of witnesses who lived through an era or event and left for future generations the task of making sense of their accounts. The Greenhaven Press History Firsthand series invites the beginner historian to commence the process of historical investigation by focusing on the words of those individuals who made history by living through it and recording their experiences firsthand.

Introduction

Between 1750 and 1850, pioneers pushed America's borders from a few colonies on the Atlantic all the way to California and Oregon on the Pacific. The new nation ultimately encompassed more than 3 million square miles. This vast territory, with its rich natural resources, made America the world power it is today.

During the 1700s the American colonies extended only about two hundred miles inland from the Atlantic coast. For the previous 150 years, the early colonial settlers had ventured no farther west than the Appalachian Mountains. These mountains were a natural barrier that stopped colonial expansion. Only fur traders and trappers traveled into the wilderness of the Ohio Valley. Native American tribes like the Ottawa, who lived west of the mountains also violently opposed any settlement in their territory. Indian attacks pushed the early pioneers back to the eastern side of the mountains.

But the lure of free land was great. So, in 1750, in spite of the danger of hostile Indian attacks, thousands of settlers began crossing the Allegheny Mountains into Pennsylvania and started farming around the present-day city of Pittsburgh. Between 1750 and 1800, pioneers pushed the frontier farther west—all the way to the Mississippi River—as they rushed into the Ohio and the Mississippi Valleys.

Culture, Motivation, and Character

The pioneers who made the difficult journey west were eager for material success. They wanted land for farming and new homes. During the colonial period, the Northeast had become overpopulated and land was becoming scarce. Sons faced the division of family farms into parcels too small to make a living. They went west to find enough land to make their own homes. Their sons often did the same thing. In the South, the cash crops of cotton and tobacco quickly depleted the soil. The plantation system, with its cheap slave labor, put many small farmers out of business and on the trail west.

The frontier represented a future of unlimited possibilities for pioneers. It was a place where they could start fresh and make new lives. Because of their isolation in the wilderness, the pioneers became less reliant on cities and on imported goods from Europe. They became more self-sufficient and less dependent on government. They were optimistic. The pioneer believed he was the equal of any man, no matter what his wealth or status.

Pioneers were lured west by promises of a paradise on Earth. In reality, though, they entered a land that was far from an Eden. They had to endure accidents, droughts, blizzards, epidemics, and starvation. They not only suffered great hardships as they moved west, but they also caused great suffering in others. The pioneers had little regard for the native peoples who already lived in North America. They felt they were superior to the Indians and had the God-given right to take Indian land for their own. Although the westward migration made the United States a stronger nation, it had a decidedly destructive effect on the Native American way of life.

The pioneers carried with them a cultural outlook and a way of life that was mainly English. This Anglo-American viewpoint would come to overwhelm and dominate not only Native American peoples but also the cultures of the French and Spanish who had also staked a claim in North America during the sixteenth, seventeenth, and eighteenth centuries.

Whether the pioneers suffered poverty and defeat or succeeded in building their ideal homes, those who journeyed to the frontier were changed by the experience and in turn changed the land around them. The pioneers were a force for good and ill. They shaped both American democracy and the character of its people as they moved into the wilderness.

Through the Cumberland Gap to Kentucky

As early as 1750, Dr. Thomas Walker discovered a gateway through the Appalachian Mountains, which he named the Cumberland Gap. This discovery was the key to opening up the Ohio Valley for settlement. However, Walker was unable to find the fabled Blue Grass country that he had heard about from the Indians. It would be up to the famous hunter and frontiersman Daniel Boone to explore the area and establish the first settlement in Kentucky. In 1775 Boone led a party through the Cumberland Gap. With thirty axmen, he blazed a trail to the Kentucky River. This trail became known as the Wilderness Trail.

After completing the trail, Boone founded a fortified town on the shore of the Kentucky River. Boone was hired to build the road and the settlement of Boonesborough by Judge Richard Henderson. Henderson dreamed of establishing a proprietary colony to which he could attract settlers and sell them plots of land on which to build their homes. This colony was to be called Transylvania. Henderson bought a huge tract of land from the Cherokee Indians. It stretched from the Cumberland Gap to the Kentucky River. Henderson's colony ultimately failed. The very road he built to bring settlers into the region was partly his undoing. Thousands of pioneers came into Kentucky on the trail Henderson had hired Boone to blaze. However, once there, many refused to buy land from him. In addition, these woodsmen would not obey the rules and regulations of Hen-

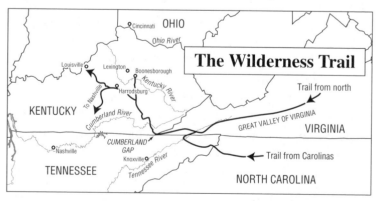

The Wilderness Trail

derson's Transylvania Colony. They settled where they chose and did what they wanted. Henderson could do nothing to stop them.

As pioneers poured into Kentucky, the Shawnee became resentful of this invasion of their hunting territory. Shawnee attacks on fortified towns like Boonesborough soon erupted into a full-scale war. The Virginia military stepped in, and after a ferocious battle, the Shawnee retreated across the Ohio River. A peace treaty was signed, and the Shawnee were forced to give up their hunting rights in Kentucky. As American and European settlers pushed farther and farther west, this pattern of Indian attacks, retaliation by the white military, and peace treaties forcing the Indians to give up their lands would repeat itself all the way to the Pacific Ocean.

The Louisiana Purchase

Just because settlers moved into a new area, that did not make the land officially part of the United States. Thus, as people moved west, the American government was also looking west to expand the borders of the new nation. For many years Thomas Jefferson had dreamed of exploring the vast territory between the Mississippi River and the Pacific Ocean. As president, Jefferson also knew that if America was to expand and prosper it would need the Mississippi River as a vital artery of commerce. He sent James Madison to help negotiate a deal with Napoléon, the emperor of France, who owned the Louisiana territory. In April 1803 the deal was struck. America got Louisiana, the entire Mississippi Valley, and New Orleans for $15 million. The Louisiana Purchase not only doubled the size of the United States but also made it almost inevitable that America would expand its borders to the Pacific Ocean.

The Louisiana Purchase encompassed an enormous territory, but neither France nor America was sure of its geographical boundaries or what lay within them. For years rumors had spread of a waterway in which boats could easily sail from the Mississippi to the Pacific. Jefferson commanded his secretary, Meriwether Lewis, to lead an expedi-

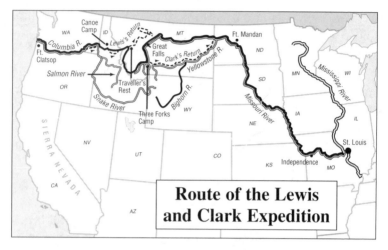

Route of the Lewis and Clark Expedition

tion to explore the rivers flowing through the Louisiana Purchase looking for the legendary Northwest Passage. Lewis chose a friend from the army, William Clark, as his cocommander. Their mission was to find the water route to the Pacific. They were also to map the area, establish friendly relations with the Native Americans, and record the plants and animals of the region.

Lewis and Clark did not find the Northwest Passage. They did, however, map the area, gather an enormous amount of scientific information, establish diplomatic and trade relations with Native American tribes, and opened the West to the great wave of migration that was to begin two decades later.

Lewis and Clark's team was one of several government-sponsored expeditions. From 1805 to 1806, Zebulon M. Pike explored and mapped the central Great Plains and the Rocky Mountains. During the 1840s John C. Frémont explored areas where others had been before him. He wrote accounts of his travels and precisely mapped the Great Plains, Rocky Mountains, Sierra Nevada, and California. When his diaries were published, they both educated people and stirred up great interest in making the trip west.

In addition to these government agents, trappers and mountain men traveled far west in search of furs. During the 1820s and 1830s they did much to explore and map the vast wilderness west of the Mississippi River. They were the first to show that wagons could be used to cross the Great Plains. As the pioneers began to make their way to California and Oregon, these men often served as guides for the wagon parties. One mountain man, James P. Beckwourth, discovered an important pass through the Sierra Nevada into northern California. He guided the first wagon train along this trail in 1850. Another famous trapper, Jedediah Smith, trekked over sixteen thousand miles across the Rocky Mountains and the Great Salt Lake into California. He provided the government valuable information and maps of the region.

Population Explosion at Home and Abroad

The push westward during the early 1800s was fueled by very high birthrates. The 1800 census recorded a population of over 5 million. By 1810 it had jumped to over 7 million—a 36 percent increase. By 1820 the population was approaching 10 million, almost doubling in twenty years. A great flood of emigrants from Europe further increased the country's population explosion. In Europe, food shortages, wars, and oppressive taxes combined with their own population explosion to produce a huge outflow of people to the United States. In 1821 the Irish potato crop failed—the first of many such failures, with the worst occurring during the 1840s. By the end of the 1840s, almost one-third of the Irish population had come to America. The British organized a sealift to Canada and America at almost no charge to the desperate Irish farmers. As these Irish emigrants poured into America's harbors, many could not find jobs or housing. They had to keep moving west into the Ohio and Mississippi Valleys.

It was the promise of cheap land that brought many from Europe to the American frontier. The Homestead Act of 1862 as well as earlier land acts put the purchase of a family farm well within the reach of millions of European and American workers and farmers. In the years after 1815, more people purchased land at cheap prices than at any other time in the history of the world.

Treaties with Native Americans in the Midwest

During the 1820s and 1830s the land between the Appalachians and the Mississippi became settled. The former frontier states of Kentucky, Ohio, and Tennessee were becoming as civilized as the eastern states. As more pioneers moved into the areas of present-day Illinois, Indiana, Michigan, and Louisiana, the federal government began making treaties with the Native American tribes in these areas. The treaties forced the Indians to give up their land and move west of the Mississippi. This policy was said to protect the Indians and their way of life, but it also opened up rich farmland for new settlers. At this time, the area west of the Mississippi, where the Indians were to be relocated, was considered a worthless desert and not suitable for farming.

By the end of 1821 the federal government controlled most of Illinois, Indiana, and Michigan. Pioneers were coming in from the east attracted by the fertile soil. They traveled from Kentucky and Tennessee, Georgia and the Carolinas. They came by wagon along the National Road running through southern Pennsylvania, central Ohio, Indiana, and Illinois. They could also take keelboats down the Ohio River, which ran along the borders of Ohio and Kentucky, and into the Mississippi River. This wave of pioneers convinced the government that even more Indian land should be opened for settlement. Starting in 1825, the government pursued a policy of Indian removal. Tribes were systematically forced to give up their territorial lands and to relocate to new lands west of the Mississippi.

In the West, the land north of the Platte River, in the present-day states of Nebraska and Wyoming, was to be the home of Native Americans already living there. South of the Platte was to be the home of the relocated eastern tribes. The treaties granted these territories to the Indians for "as long as the grass grows and the rivers run." But waves of future pioneers and the government would break these treaties again and again.

Manifest Destiny

Between 1845 and 1848 the United States expanded its territory over 1 million square miles. This was more land than was acquired in the Louisiana Purchase. The government gained this huge amount of territory through a variety of means—annexation, peaceful diplomacy, and war.

The United States annexed Texas in 1845. Texas had already won its independence from Mexico in 1836 during a series of battles during the Texas revolution. Texas thereby became an independent state. It then began petitioning to become part of the United States. The question of whether to admit Texas to the Union was debated by Congress and the White House for ten years before President James K. Polk, who had run on an expansionist ticket, signed the proclamation making Texas the twenty-eighth state.

During the 1840s American pioneers were beginning to migrate to the choice farming country in Oregon. This area was formally claimed by Britain. In 1846, however, President Polk negotiated a treaty with Britain that gave the United States the territory that would later become the states of Oregon, Washington, and Idaho. Before the treaty, America had claimed all of the land up to the present-day boundary of Alaska, which was then owned by Russia. The British claimed territory from Alaska to as far south as the Columbia River in Oregon. President Polk was able to work out a compromise. The treaty established the border at the forty-ninth parallel, which is the present boundary of Washington and British Columbia, Canada. The compromise successfully avoided another war with Britain.

Polk, however, was unable to avoid conflict with another neighbor. The annexation of Texas provoked a war with Mexico. Polk not only accepted Texas into the Union, but he also set the southern border of Texas at the Rio Grande— 150 miles south of the accepted Texas-Mexico dividing line. This was the provocation that set off almost two years of fighting between Mexican and American armies. The American forces finally occupied Mexico City, ending the war. In 1848 the Treaty of Guadalupe Hidalgo was signed. The

United States paid Mexico $15 million and was ceded a huge parcel of land that included the present-day states of Texas, New Mexico, Arizona, California, Nevada, Utah, Colorado, and Wyoming.

A month before the signing of the Treaty of Guadalupe Hidalgo, the first traces of gold were discovered around Sacramento, California, by employees of John Sutter. Sutter, an early pioneer, rancher, and promoter of California settlement, was not happy about the discovery because he thought gold seekers would trample his land. He tried to keep the discovery a secret, but the news quickly got out and set off the gold rush of 1849. During the next few years hundreds of thousands of prospectors traveled to the gold fields in one of the most amazing population movements in history. Between 1848 and 1852 the population of California jumped from 14,000 to 250,000. With this huge influx of people, California became the thirty-first state of the Union, just two years after the gold rush began. As John Sutter had suspected, the massive immigration brought on by the gold rush overwhelmed the area. Hispanics and Native Americans were especially hard hit. White settlers took land from many Hispanics. They hunted down and killed Native Americans. In their search for gold and land, prospectors and settlers were an unstoppable and often destructive force.

Few prospectors or pioneers questioned their right to move into Texas, Oregon, or California, even when other countries owned these territories. Many believed in expanding democracy and freedom to others. Some said that the American ethic of hard work and economic progress should triumph over the outmoded monarchy of Britain and the instability of Mexico. The pioneers believed that it was not only inevitable but also ordained by God that the United States should rule North America. In 1845 a New York newspaper writer, John L. O'Sullivan, gave these beliefs a name. In an editorial arguing for the annexation of Texas, he coined the term *manifest destiny*. The phrase was picked up by politicians, who used it to justify making California, Oregon, and Alaska part of the United States.

Oregon and California Bound

Even as late as 1840, it seemed to many that the Mississippi River would remain the boundary of the frontier for many years to come. At that time the land just west of the Mississippi was thought to be mostly desert and not good for farming. Because of this misconception, many people interested in moving west did not want to settle there. They wanted to keep going, attracted by the glowing reports of fertile lands beyond the desert—all the way to California and Oregon.

In 1845 only twenty thousand white Americans lived west of the Mississippi. Much of the activity in this region centered on the fur trade. During the 1830s most of the fertile farmland had been claimed in the Midwest. This left many people looking for other places to settle. In 1830 a company of fur traders—Smith, Jackson, and Sublette—moved their furs by wagons to a trading fair in the Rocky Mountains. They proved that a wagon train could make the journey across the plains. Two years later, in 1832, Hall Jackson Kelley led a small party of pioneers to Oregon. One of the members of this party was Nathaniel J. Wyeth. Wyeth formed a company and led an expedition across the continent. His party was the first to travel over what would become the Oregon Trail that crossed the western half of the

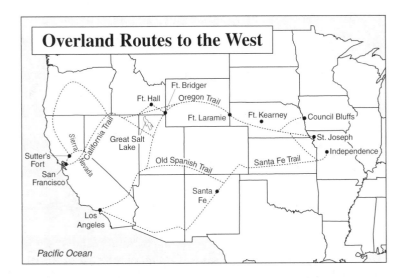

Overland Routes to the West

country from Missouri to Oregon.

In 1842 one of America's most famous explorers, John Charles Frémont, with his guide, Kit Carson, made a detailed map of the Oregon Trail. This map showed campsites, mountain passes, and watering holes. Frémont's report of the expedition became a best-seller. Now that the route had been mapped and publicized, more and more people were willing to make the journey across the plains to the Pacific.

Many pioneers were persuaded to make the overland trip to California and Oregon by advertisements and letters from explorers and early settlers. One early settler, Thomas O. Larkin, the U.S. consul in California, was a regular correspondent for major newspapers in New York and Boston. Larkin's letters were full of practical tips about moving to the Pacific coast—equipment for the journey, what to do when you arrived in Sacramento, and the best crops for the California climate. For many pioneers, these newspaper articles became their travel guide to the West Coast.

The Great Migration

In 1843 Congress was considering a bill that would allow every adult male settler in the Pacific Northwest to claim 640 acres of land. He could also claim 160 for each child and 160 for his wife. That spring, with the promise of these land grants, more than one thousand pioneers left Independence, Missouri, on the 2,000-mile trail to Oregon. By 1846 many thousands of pioneers were moving west.

Most pioneers began their journey at one of the jumping-off towns along the Missouri River. The trail followed the Platte River in Nebraska to Fort Laramie in Wyoming and across the mountains of the Continental Divide at South Pass. In the southwest corner of Wyoming, the wagon trains could stop to buy supplies and rest at Fort Bridger. This was actually a trading post built by the trapper Jim Bridger, who charged travelers very high prices at this frontier convenience store.

Up to this point the trip was relatively easy. After Fort Bridger, however, the trail divided: One trail headed north through Idaho and into Oregon, and the other headed south through Nevada and into Sacramento, California. On both routes pioneers faced deserts and treacherous mountain trails. Furniture, iron stoves, and even the wagons themselves were sometimes abandoned to lighten the load. Food and water frequently ran out. Cattle died from thirst in the desert and the endurance of the travelers was pushed to the limits. The journey took between five and six months, and timing was very important. The wagons had to make it through the western mountain ranges before the winter snows set in. If they started their journey too late in the spring or were delayed along the way, they could get stranded and face the same terrible fate that claimed so many of the Donner Party in 1846—death and starvation.

Many dangers and difficulties existed along the trail. Rivers had to be crossed and recrossed. Accidents were common: Between 1840 and 1860 almost three hundred pioneers died by drowning. Water was always a problem for the pioneers. If they started too early, the spring rains would bog the wagons down in mud. Further along, the plains became unbearably hot and dry. Cattle died of thirst or stampeded when they finally caught the scent of water. Watering holes often turned out to be poisoned. Hundreds of travelers died from cholera contracted from contaminated wells. Floods, hail, and lightning were also problems, as was the threat of early snows. But despite all of these dangers and because of their great determination, most pioneers made it to their destination and built their new homes.

Encountering Native Americans in the West

As the pioneers crossed the western plains to California and Oregon, the Indians they encountered were at first helpful and friendly. The Indians guided pioneer wagon trains through mountain passes and across rivers. The pioneers traded with them for horses and food. But as had happened in Kentucky, the Indians became resentful as the great numbers of settlers began to overrun their lands. The pioneers killed their buffalo for food. Cattle overgrazed the grass and drank up the watering holes. Farmers took Indian land and cut down the trees. Many Indians came to believe that they must fight these invaders or face the total annihilation of their way of life. Some tribes charged tolls for passing through Indian territory. The pioneers thought the Indians had no right to charge these tolls and often refused to pay. The Indians would then steal the settlers' cattle and other goods as payment.

In 1852 the Pawnee had set up a toll bridge over a creek. A pioneer wagon train refused to pay the toll of twenty-five cents per wagon and rushed onto the bridge. But the Indians had camouflaged a hole in the middle of the bridge, and the lead wagon plunged into the water. Gunfire erupted, and nine Pawnee were killed. Newspapers wrote about such incidents and exaggerated events to make a good story. The truth was that Native Americans killed relatively few pioneers who moved west. The real dangers to the pioneers were accidents and disease, which killed almost ten thousand settlers between 1840 and 1860. But such facts were useless to newspapermen wanting to sell papers or to politicians wanting more land to sell.

There were, however, some savage and bloody battles. In 1854 thirty Snake Indians attacked a small wagon train over an argument about a horse and killed eighteen members of the expedition. This attack caused an uproar in the press. The editor of Portland's *Weekly Oregonian* demanded the army "exterminate the race of Indians."

As the violence escalated, atrocities were committed on both sides. In 1862 the Sioux killed 500 settlers in Minnesota. In turn, the government hanged 38 Sioux leaders. In 1864 the U.S. military massacred 450 Indians at Sand Creek, Colorado. Usually it was the Indians who came out worse in these fights. The government tried to solve the conflicts by making treaties with the various tribes. These treaties required the Indians to abandon their nomadic way of life and live on permanent reservations. The Indians also had to agree not to attack the settlers. In return, the Indians received annual government payments.

Homesteading the Plains

With the buffalo gone and the Indians removed to the reservations, the Great Plains were open for settlers. Congress wanted to encourage farming in the western states, and in 1862 it passed the Homestead Act. This law provided a family with 160 acres of public land if they stayed for five years. The government offered further assistance with the Timber Culture Act of 1873. It provided that a settler could claim an additional 160 acres of public land if he planted forty acres in trees and raised them for eight years. Because of these laws, more American land was put in cultivation between 1870 and 1890 than the entire 250 years since the landing at Jamestown in 1607.

The Great Plains had been considered a desert and unsuitable for farming. The area was largely passed over for the Pacific coast by the great migrations of the 1840s and 1850s. When this land was claimed and used up, the sons of farmers began to look to the vast open prairies to start their own farms. They discovered that underneath the prairie grass was a fertile black earth that could be plowed and productively planted.

Although prairie land was cheap and plentiful, the problems the plains pioneers faced were many. Because of the scarcity of water, farmers had to learn new methods of dry farming. To break up the tough prairie sod, a farmer needed a special steel plow pulled by at least three oxen. With this team, a settler could plow only one or two acres a day.

For Mormon settlers, the first years of farming were especially difficult. The land around Salt Lake, where they had settled, was a desert. No trees grew there. To construct their houses, wood had to be hauled with great effort from nearby mountains. Very little rain fell, and before crops could be planted, an extensive system of irrigation canals had to be dug.

In 1873 farmers were hit by a grasshopper plague. The insects came in great clouds and destroyed the crops. Bark on trees, lumber on house walls, and clothes hanging on clothes lines were also devoured. Even trains were stopped because the thick carpet of grasshoppers made the tracks as slick as if they had been greased.

Daily Life

Cut off from civilization, the pioneers had to rely on themselves and their own hard work to live off the land they had claimed. The pioneers had to produce almost all of the necessities of life. They had to build furniture and make their own clothing. Self-reliance became part of their character, and this often carried them through the trials of daily life.

For many of the pioneers, bad sanitation, poor diet, constant hard work, and exposure to the harsh climate produced a lot of disease and illness, such as dysentery, cholera, smallpox, and typhoid. Doctors were scarce, and settlers often relied on home remedies to combat their ills. The life of a pioneer woman was especially hard. She worked eighteen hours a day and was always tired. She spent her entire life alone in the house, often not seeing her nearest neighbor for several months. She had very little support, even during childbirth. The hard work, severe weather, and successive pregnancies made her look old by thirty.

The life of a pioneer farmer was always risky. Some settlers lost their crops when they had to flee from wars with the Indians. Others lost their entire homestead in legal disputes over the claim to their land. There was always a lack of water. There were fires, floods, blizzards, dust storms, and tornadoes. Pioneers had come two thousand miles in search of an ideal home. Many people were broken by the difficult life in the wilderness and went back east. But many more endured and prospered. The pioneers needed all of their courage and resourcefulness to survive. For many, it would take a lifetime to accomplish their goals.

In 1890 the Census Bureau announced that the frontier was closed. The boundary line between settlement and frontier could no longer be drawn. The rapid settlement of the last frontier, the Great Plains, with a large population of pioneers and farmers, had tamed the wilderness. There were still pockets of free land to be had, especially in Oklahoma, where land rushes occurred until 1911, but after 1890 the vast uncharted territory that had once been western America no longer existed.

The Importance of the Pioneers

The story of the pioneers and the great westward movement is one of the key events that shaped the American people and its democracy. The pioneers faced a great challenge in settling the unknown frontier. It brought out the best and sometimes the worst in their character. Their struggles and strength of character have left an indelible mark on American society. Even in the present day, the pioneer spirit shapes the outlook of America. Americans are always striving to be on the forefront of the frontier, whether it be in technology, science, or art. Their restless quest keeps pushing back the frontiers of the ocean and of outer space. Modern-day pioneers still want to explore the unknown, from the subatomic world of atoms to the farthest worlds of the galaxy. As Americans look back at the bravery and determination of the pioneers, they have much to learn from them as the nation continues to travel into future frontiers.

Chapter 1

The Pathfinders

Chapter Preface

The United States did not always stretch from the Atlantic to the Pacific. For well over a century, the first immigrants who came to North America settled along the Atlantic coast. The natural barrier of the Appalachian Mountains kept these early colonial settlements from expanding. But there were always some explorers, hunters, and traders who ventured into unknown regions. They brought back stories of the wonders of the lands to the west. As the East Coast became more densely populated, game became scarcer and crops began to fail as the soil lost its fertility. People needed more room, and Kentucky became the next great destination for expansion. John Filson, the author of the *Adventures of Colonel Daniel Boone,* wrote that Kentucky flowed "with milk and honey . . . a land of wheat and barley, and all kinds of fruits. You shall eat bread without scarceness, and not lack anything in it."

But before the settlers could reach this promised land, passes through the mountains needed to be discovered, trails for horses and wagons needed to be cut, and friendly relations with the Native Americans needed to be established. This was the job of the pathfinders. It was up to them to lead the way and push back the barriers of the frontier.

Daniel Boone led one of the first expeditions through the Cumberland Gap in the Appalachians in 1775. This was the first trickle of what would become a flood of pioneers traveling west. The great migration would culminate in the 1840s and 1850s as pioneers crossed the plains into Kansas, Texas, California, and Oregon. But just as the Appalachians were a barrier to the early colonialist, the Rockies and Sierras stood as even greater natural obstacles for the pioneers. It would again be up to the pathfinders to chart the way across the plains and the snowcapped Continental Divide.

Meriwether Lewis and William Clark took up the challenge in 1804 after President Thomas Jefferson bought the eight-hundred-thousand-square-mile territory of Louisiana from France. This was a vast region that was larger than the United States at that time. Few Europeans had traveled in this unknown land. It was up to Lewis and Clark to map this region, find a route to the Pacific, and establish trade with the Indians.

In 1842 another great pathfinder, John C. Frémont, made an accurate map of the Oregon Trail detailing campsites, water holes, and passes through the mountains. James P. Beckwourth, an African American fur trader and scout, discovered an important pass through the Sierras and guided the first wagon train through in 1850. These great explorers also published accounts of their adventures. These books often became best-sellers and inspired in people in the East and in the Ohio Valley to make their preparations for the move west.

Daniel Boone Builds and Defends Boonesborough

John Filson

During colonial times, the frontier was still east of the Appalachian Mountains. Knowing that unexplored land lay to the west of this barrier, certain business interests employed guides to lead settlers into these unclaimed regions and develop the land. A lawyer, Richard Henderson, and the Transylvania Company hired one such guide, Daniel Boone, to cross the Appalachians and open up Kentucky and establish it as the fourteenth colony. Native Americans were known to inhabit the western lands and Boone negotiated a treaty with the Cherokees in which he bought 20 million acres of unseen land. Boone then led a party of settlers from Tennessee through the Cumberland Gap in the Appalachians and established the town of Boonesborough in Kentucky.

But the treaty with the Cherokees had left out other tribes living in the area like the warlike Shawnee. The Shawnee feared that the white settlers would soon overrun their hunting grounds. To make matters worse, the American Revolution was beginning and many of the southern Indian tribes allied themselves with the British. The disgruntled tribes used their new British rifles on the settlers. Through continual fighting, the new territory of Kentucky soon earned the nickname "the dark and bloody ground."

Despite these conflicts at least seventy thousand people

Excerpted from *The Discovery and Settlement of Kentucke,* by John Filson (Ann Arbor: MI: University Microfilms, 1966).

traveled the Wilderness Road blazed by Boone between 1775 and 1795. These were the first pioneers. They filled the Ohio River Valley, the lower Mississippi Valley, and eventually Illinois, Indiana and Michigan.

In this autobiographical narrative, Daniel Boone tells the story of his struggles in 1775 to lead a party of settlers along the Wilderness Road and establish the town of Boonesborough. Because Boone was too busy to write about his own life, he told his stories to John Filson who wrote the book that held this account. When asked if the book was true, Boone winked and said, "All true. . . . Not a lie in it!" Boone's published adventures are part of the mythologizing of the west. Books about the heroic deeds of the pioneers played an important role in attracting people to settle in unknown western lands.

I sold my farm on the Yadkin, and what goods we could not carry with us; and on the twenty-fifth day of September, 1773, bade a farewell to our friends, and proceeded on our journey to Kentucky, in company with five families more, and forty men that joined us in Powel's Valley, which is one hundred and fifty miles from the now settled parts of Kentucky.

This promising beginning was soon overcast with a cloud of adversity; for upon the tenth day of October, the rear of our company was attacked by a number of Indians, who killed six, and wounded one man. Of these my eldest son was one that fell in the action. Though we defended ourselves, and repulsed the enemy, yet this unhappy affair scattered our cattle, brought us into extreme difficulty, and so discouraged the whole company, that we retreated forty miles, to the settlement on Clinch River.

We had passed over two mountains, viz. Powel's and Walden's, and were approaching Cumberland mountain when this adverse fortune overtook us. These mountains are in the wilderness, as we pass from the old settlements in Virginia to Kentucky, are ranged in a S.W. and N.E. direction, are of a great length and breadth, and not far distant from each other. Over these, nature hath formed passes that are less difficult than might be expected from a view of such huge piles. The aspect of these cliffs is so wild and horrid, that it is impossible to behold them without terror. . . .

I remained with my family on Clinch until the sixth of June 1774, when I and one Michael Stoner were solicited by Governor Dunmore of Virginia, to go to the Falls of the Ohio, to conduct into the settlement a number of surveyors that had been sent thither by him some months before; this country having about this time drawn the attention of many adventurers. We immediately complied with the Governor's request, and conducted in the surveyors, compleating a tour of eight hundred miles, through many difficulties, in sixty-two days.

Building Boonesborough

I soon began this work, having collected a number of enterprising men, well armed. We proceeded with all possible expedition until we came within fifteen miles of where Boonesborough now stands, and where we were fired upon by a party of Indians that killed two, and wounded two of our number; yet, although surprised and taken at a disadvantage, we stood our ground. This was on the twentieth of March, 1775. Three days after, we were fired upon again, and had two men killed, and three wounded. Afterwards we proceeded on to Kentucky River without opposition; and on the first day of April began to erect the fort of Boonesborough at a salt lick, about sixty yards from the river, on the S. side.

On the fourth day, the Indians killed one of our men. We were busily employed in building this fort, until the fourteenth day of June following, without any further opposition from the Indians; and having finished the works, I returned to my family, on Clinch.

In a short time, I proceeded to remove my family from Clinch to this garrison; where we arrived safe without any other difficulties than such as are common to this passage, my wife and daughter being the first white women that ever stood on the banks of Kentucky River.

On the twenty-fourth day of December following, we had one man killed, and one wounded, by the Indians, who seemed determined to persecute us for erecting this fortification.

On the fourteenth day of July 1776, two of Col. Callaway's daughters, and one of mine, were taken prisoners near the fort. I immediately pursued the Indians, with only eight men, and on the sixteenth overtook them, killed two of the party, and recovered the girls. The same day on which this attempt was made, the Indians divided themselves into different parties, and attacked several forts, which were shortly before this time erected, doing a great deal of mischief.

This was extremely distressing to the new settlers. The innocent husbandman was shot down, while busy in cultivating the soil for his family's supply. Most of the cattle around the stations were destroyed. They continued their hostilities in this manner until the fifteenth of April 1777, when they attacked Boonesborough with a party of above one hundred in number, killed one man, and wounded four. Their loss in this attack was not certainly known to us.

Besieged

On the fourth day of July following, a party of about two hundred Indians attacked Boonesborough, killed one man, and wounded two. They besieged us forty-eight hours; during which time seven of them were killed, and, at last, finding themselves not likely to prevail, they raised the siege, and departed.

The Indians had disposed their warriors in different parties at this time, and attacked the different garrisons to prevent their assisting each other, and did much injury to the distressed inhabitants.

On the nineteenth day of this month, Col. Logan's fort was besieged by a party of about two hundred Indians. During this dreadful siege they did a great deal of mischief, distressed the garrison, in which were only fifteen men, killed two, and wounded one. The enemy's loss was uncertain, from the common practice which the Indians have of carrying off their dead in time of battle.

Col. Harrod's fort was then defended by only sixty-five

men, and Boonesborough by twenty-two, there being no more forts or white men in the country, except at the Falls, a considerable distance from these; and all taken collectively, were but a handful to the numerous warriors that were everywhere dispersed through the country, intent upon doing all the mischief that savage barbarity could invent. Thus we passed through a scene of sufferings that exceeds description.

On the twenty-fifth of this month, a reinforcement of forty-five men arrived from North Carolina, and about the twentieth of August following, Col. Bowman arrived with one hundred men from Virginia. Now we began to strengthen, and from hence, for the space of six weeks, we had skirmishes with Indians, in one quarter or other, almost every day.

The savages now learned the superiority of the Long Knife, as they call the Virginians, by experience; being outgeneralled in almost every battle. Our affairs began to wear a new aspect, and the enemy, not daring to venture on open war, practiced secret mischief at times.

Captured

On the first day of January 1778, I went with a party of thirty men to the Blue Licks, on Licking River, to make salt for the different garrisons in the country.

On the 7th day of February, as I was hunting to procure meat for the company, I met with a party of one hundred and two Indians, and two Frenchmen, on their march against Boonesborough, that place being particularly the object of the enemy.

They pursued, and took me; and brought me on the eighth day to the Licks, where twenty-seven of my party were, three of them having previously returned home with the salt. I, knowing it was impossible for them to escape, capitulated with the enemy, and, at a distance in their view, gave notice to my men of their situation, with orders not to resist, but surrender themselves captives.

The generous usage the Indians had promised before in my capitulation, was afterwards fully complied with, and we proceeded with them as prisoners to old Chelicothe, the principal Indian town on Little Miami, where we arrived, after an uncomfortable journey in very severe weather, on the eighteenth day of February, and received as good treatment as prisoners could expect from savages. On the tenth day of March following, I and the rest of my men were conducted by forty Indians to Detroit, where we arrived the thirtieth day, and were treated by Governor Hamilton, the British commander at that post, with great humanity.

During our travels, the Indians entertained me well; and their affection for me was so great, that they utterly refused to leave me there with the others, although the Governor offered them one hundred pounds sterling for me, on purpose to give me a parole to go home. Several English gentlemen there, being sensible of my adverse fortune, and touched with human sympathy, generously offered a friendly supply for my wants, which I refused, with many thanks for their kindness; adding, that I never expected it would be in my power to recompense such unmerited generosity.

With the Shawnee

The Indians left my men in captivity with the British at Detroit, and on the tenth day of April brought me towards Old Chelicothe, where we arrived on the twenty-fifth day of the same month. This was a long and fatiguing march, through an exceeding fertile country, remarkable for fine springs and streams of water. At Chelicothe I spent my time as comfortably as I could expect; was adopted, according to their custom, into a family, where I became a son, and had a great share in the affection of my new parents, brothers, sisters, and friends. I was exceedingly familiar and friendly with them, always appearing as cheerful and satisfied as possible, and they put great confidence in me.

I often went a hunting with them, and frequently gained their applause for my activity at our shooting-matches. I was careful not to exceed many of them in shooting; for no people are more envious than they in this sport. I could observe, in their countenances and gestures, the greatest expressions of joy when they exceeded me; and, when the reverse happened, of envy.

The Shawanese king took great notice of me, and treated me with profound respect, and entire friendship, often entrusting me to hunt at my liberty. I frequently returned with the spoils of the woods, and as often presented some of what I had taken to him, expressive of duty to my sovereign. My food and lodging were in common with them; not so good indeed as I could desire, but necessity made every thing acceptable. . . .

When I returned to Chelicothe, alarmed to see four hundred and fifty Indians, of their choicest warriors, painted and armed in a fearful manner, ready to march against Boonesborough, I determined to escape the first opportunity.

On the sixteenth, before sun-rise, I departed in the most secret manner, and arrived at Boonesborough on the twentieth, after a journey of one hundred and sixty miles; during which, I had but one meal.

I found our fortress in a bad state of defence; but we proceeded immediately to repair our flanks, strengthen our gates and posterns, and form double bastions, which we completed in ten days. In this time we daily expected the arrival of the Indian army; and at length, one of my fellow prisoners, escaping from them, arrived, informing us that the enemy had, on account of my departure, postponed their expedition three weeks.

The Indians had spies out viewing our movements, and were greatly alarmed with our increase in number and fortifications. The Grand Councils of the nations were held frequently, and with more deliberation than usual. They evidently saw the approaching hour when the Long Knife would dispossess them of their desirable habitations; and, anxiously concerned for futurity, determined utterly to extirpate the whites out of Kentucky. We were not intimidated by their movements, but frequently gave them proofs of our courage. . . .

On the eighth [of August], the Indian army arrived, being four hundred and forty-four in number, commanded by Capt.

Duquesne, eleven other Frenchmen, and some of their own chiefs, and marched up within view of our fort, with British and French colours flying; and having sent a summons to me, in his Britannick Majesty's name, to surrender the fort, I requested two days consideration, which was granted.

It was now a critical period with us. We were a small number in the garrison: a powerful army before our walls, whose appearance proclaimed inevitable death, fearfully painted, and marking their footsteps with desolation. Death was preferable to captivity; and if taken by storm, we must inevitably be devoted to destruction. In this situation we concluded to maintain our garrison, if possible.

We immediately proceeded to collect what we could of our horses, and other cattle, and bring them through the posterns into the fort: and in the evening of the ninth, I returned answer, that we were determined to defend our fort while a man was living.

"Now," said I to their commander, who stood attentively hearing my sentiments, "We laugh at all your formidable preparations: but thank you for giving us notice and time to provide for our defence. Your efforts will not prevail; for our gates shall for ever deny you admittance."

Whether this answer affected their courage, or not, I cannot tell; but, contrary to our expectations, they formed a scheme to deceive us, declaring it was their orders, from Governor Hamilton, to take us captives, and not to destroy us; but if nine of us would come out, and treat with them, they would immediately withdraw their forces from our walls, and return home peaceably. This sounded grateful in our ears; and we agreed to the proposal.

We held the treaty within sixty yards of the garrison, on purpose to divert them from a breach of honour, as we could not avoid suspicions of the savages. In this situation the articles were formally agreed to, and signed; and the Indians told us it was customary with them, on such occasions, for two Indians to shake hands with every white man in the treaty, as an evidence of entire friendship. We agreed to this also, but were soon convinced their policy was to take us prisoners.

They immediately grappled us; but, although surrounded by hundreds of savages, we extricated ourselves from them, and escaped all safe into the garrison, except one that was wounded, through a heavy fire from their army. They immediately attacked us on every side, and a constant heavy fire ensued between us, day and night, for the space of nine days.

In this time the enemy began to undermine our fort, which was situated sixty yards from Kentucky River. They began at the water-mark, and proceeded in the bank some distance, which we understood by their making the water muddy with the clay; and we immediately proceeded to disappoint their design, by cutting a trench across their subterranean passage. The enemy discovering our counter-mine, by the clay we threw out of the fort, desisted from that stratagem: and experience now fully convincing them that neither their power nor policy could effect their purpose, on the twentieth day of August they raised the siege, and departed.

During this siege, which threatened death in every form, we had two men killed, and four wounded, besides a number of cattle. We killed of the enemy thirty-seven, and wounded a great number. After they were gone, we picked up one hundred and twenty-five pounds weight of bullets, besides what stuck in the logs of our fort; which certainly is a great proof of their industry.

Soon after this, I went into the settlement, and nothing worthy of a place in this account passed in my affairs for some time.

Lewis and Clark Explore the Northwest Territory

Meriwether Lewis and William Clark

For many years, President Thomas Jefferson had dreamed of sending an expedition to explore the vast area of North America between the Mississippi and the Pacific. With the Louisiana Purchase in 1803, Jefferson's dream became a practical reality. The president sent Captains Meriwether Lewis and William Clark on a mission to assert America's authority in the newly acquired Northwest Territories. Their mission also included establishing friendly relations with the Native American tribes and finding a trade route to the Pacific coast. The Lewis and Clark Expedition departed from St. Louis on May 14, 1804, with forty-five men in two canoes and a large keelboat. The first stage of the journey, lasting 166 days and sixteen hundred miles, was through familiar territory to the Mandan Indian village in North Dakota. Here they built a fort to spend the winter. In March of 1805, a smaller force of twenty-nine headed down the Yellowstone River and into unexplored territory to find the rumored Northwest Passage, a direct water route into the new region. The party included Clark's slave York, a Shoshone Indian woman named Sacagawea, her baby, and her husband Charbonneau.

Sacagewea guided the explorers as far as the Great Falls of the Missouri River, which was as far as their boats would take

Excerpted from *The Journals of Lewis and Clark*, edited by John Bakeless (New York: Penguin Books USA Inc., 1964).

them. She then helped them get horses from the Shoshone
Indians to transport their supplies over the Rocky Mountains.
Once over the mountains, Lewis and Clark used canoes to
make their way down the Columbia River and to the Pacific
Ocean.

Although they did not find the Northwest Passage as they
had hoped, the two leaders kept records of people and
wildlife they saw that proved invaluable to eastern interests.
Furthermore, the Lewis and Clark Expedition opened up
unexplored regions of the country to a flood of settlement that
would follow two decades later.

[L ewis]   Fort Mandan, April 7th, 1805
. . . Captain Clark embarked with our party and
proceeded up the [Yellowstone] river. As I had used no exercise for several weeks, I determined to walk on shore as
far as our encampment of this evening. Accordingly I continued my walk on the north side of the river about six
miles, to the upper village of the Mandans, and called on
The Black Cat, or Posecopsehá, the Great Chief of the Mandans. He was not at home. I rested myself a few minutes
and, finding that the party had not arrived, I returned about
two miles and joined them at their encampment on the N.
side of the river opposite the lower Mandan village.

Our party now consisted of the following individuals:

Sergeants:	John Ordway	Nathaniel Pryor
	Patrick Gass	
Privates:	William Bratton	John Colter
	Reuben Fields	Joseph Fields
	John Shields	George Gibson
	George Shannon	John Potts
	John Collins	Joseph Whitehouse
	Richard Windsor	Alexander Willard
	Hugh Hall	Silas Goodrich
	Robert Frazer	Peter Cruzat
	John Baptiste Lepage	Francis Labiche
	Hugh McNeil	William Warner

Thomas P. Howard   Peter Wiser
John B. Thompson

Interpreters: George Drouilliard and Toussaint Charbonneau; also a black man by the name of York, servant to Captain Clark; an Indian woman, wife to Charbonneau, with a young child; and a Mandan man who had promised us to accompany us as far as the Snake Indians, with a view to bring about a good understanding and friendly intercourse between that nation and his own, the Minnetarees and Amahamis.

Our vessels consisted of six small canoes and two large pirogues. This little fleet, although not quite so respectable as that of Columbus or Captain Cook; was still viewed by us with as much pleasure as those deservedly famed adventurers ever beheld theirs, and, I daresay, with quite as much anxiety for their safety and preservation. We were now about to penetrate a country at least two thousand miles in width, on which the foot of civilized man had never trod. The good or evil it had in store for us was for experiment yet to determine, and these little vessels contained every article by which we were to expect to subsist or defend ourselves. However, as the state of mind in which we are, generally gives the coloring to events, when the imagination is suffered to wander into futurity, the picture which now presented itself to me was a most pleasing one.

Entertaining as I do the most confident hope of succeeding in a voyage which had formed a darling project of mine for the last ten years, I could but esteem this moment of my departure as among the most happy of my life. The party are in excellent health and spirits, zealously attached to the enterprise, and anxious to proceed. Not a whisper or murmur of discontent to be heard among them, but all act in unison and with the most perfect harmony. . . .

[As the expedition arrived in the Rocky Mountains, they could not go further in the boats. Sacagewea guided them to a Shoshone Indian village. It turned out that the chief was her brother. Lewis and Clark were able to trade with the Shoshones for the horses they needed to cross the mountains and continue to the Pacific Ocean.]

Across the Rocky Mountains

[Lewis]   August 17, 1805

This morning I arose very early and dispatched Drouil-liard and the Indian down the river. Sent Shields to hunt. I made McNeal cook the remainder of our meat, which af-forded a slight breakfast for ourselves and the chief. Drouil-liard had been gone about two hours when an Indian, who had straggled some little distance down the river, returned and reported that the white men were coming, that he had seen them just below. They all appeared transported with joy, and the chief repeated his fraternal hug. I felt quite as much gratified at this information as the Indians appeared to be. Shortly after, Captain Clark arrived with the inter-preter, Charbonneau, and the Indian woman, who proved to be a sister of the chief Cameâhwait.

The meeting of those people was really affecting, particu-larly between Sacagawea and an Indian woman who had been taken prisoner at the same time with her, and who had after-wards escaped from the Minnetarees and rejoined her nation.

At noon the canoes arrived, and we had the satisfaction once more to find ourselves all together, with a flattering prospect of being able to obtain as many horses shortly as would enable us to prosecute our voyage by land should that by water be deemed inadvisable.

We now formed our camp just below the junction of the forks on the larboard side in a level, smooth bottom covered with a fine turf of greensward. Here we unloaded our canoes and arranged our baggage on shore. Formed a canopy of one of our large sails and planted some willow brush in the ground to form a shade for the Indians to sit under while we spoke to them, which we thought it best to do this evening.

Accordingly, about 4 P.M., we called them together and through the medium of Labiche, Charbonneau, and Saca-gawea, we communicated to them fully the objects which had brought us into this distant part of the country, in which we took care to make them a conspicuous object of our own good wishes and the care of our government. We made them sensible of their dependence on the will of our government for every species of merchandise as well for their defense and comfort; and apprised them of the strength of our government and its friendly dispositions toward them. We also gave them as a reason why we wished to penetrate the country as far as the ocean to the west of them was to examine and find out a more direct way to bring merchandise to them. That as no trade could be carried on with them before our return to our homes, that it was mutually advantageous to them as well as to ourselves that they should render us such aids as they had it in their power to furnish in order to hasten our voyage and, of course, our return home: that such were their horses to transport our baggage, without which we could not subsist; and that a pilot to conduct us through the mountains was also necessary if we could not descend the river by water. But that we did not ask either their horses or their services without giving a satisfactory compensation in return. That at present we wished them to collect as many horses as were necessary to transport our baggage to their village on the Columbia, where we would then trade with them at our leisure for such horses as they could spare us. They appeared well pleased with what had been said. The chief thanked us for friendship toward himself and nation and declared his wish to serve us in every respect; that he was sorry to find that it must yet be some time before they could be furnished with firearms, but said they could live as they had done heretofore until we brought them as we had promised. He said they had not horses enough with them at present to remove our baggage to their village over the mountain, but that he would return tomorrow and encourage his people to come over with their horses, and that he would bring his own and assist us. This was complying with all we wished at present. We next inquired who were chiefs among them. Cameâhwait pointed out two others, who, he said, were chiefs. We gave him a medal of the small size with the likeness of Mr. Jefferson, the President of the United States, in relief on one side, and clasped hands with a pipe and tomahawk on the other. To the other chiefs we gave each a small

S

Our hunters killed 3 bucks, 4 brant, and 3

ng, seven Indians of the Clatsop nation came
. They brought with them two sea-otter skins,
asked blue beads &c., and such high prices
nable to purchase them without reducing our
merchandise on which we depended for sub-
return up this river. Merely to try the Indian
f those skins, I offered him my watch, hand-
ch of red beads, and a dollar of the American
hich he refused and demanded *ti-â-co-mo-*
is "chief beads," and the common blue beads,
ich we have at this time. . . .

December 3rd, 1805
y name and the day of the month and year on
ee on this peninsula:
liam Clark December 3d 1805. By Land.

U. States in 1804–1805
roke the two shank bones of the elk after the
aken out; boiled them, and extracted a pint of
ow from them. Sergeant Pryor and Gibson re-
night and informed me they had been lost the
f the time they were out, and had killed six elk
ft lying, having taken out their entrails.

December 7th, 1805
at 8 o'clock down to the place Captain Lewis
winter quarters when he was down. We stopped
the commencement of a bay, after which we pro-
round the bay to S.E. and ascended a creek 8
gh point and camped. At this place of encamp-
pose to build and pass the winter. The situation
er of, as we conceive, a hunting country.

December 8th, 1805
g fixed on this situation as the one best calcu-
winter quarters, I determined to go as direct a
could to the seacoast, which we could hear roar
d to be at no great distance from us. My princi-
to look out a place to make salt, blaze the road

medal which were struck in the Presidency of George Washington, Esq. We also gave small medals of the last description to two young men who, the first chief informed us, were good young men and much respected among them.

Captain Clark and myself now concerted measures for our future operations; and it was mutually agreed that he should set out tomorrow morning with eleven men, furnished with axes and other necessary tools for making canoes, their arms, accouterments, and as much of their baggage as they could carry, also to take the Indians, Charbonneau, and the Indian woman with him. That on his arrival at the Shoshone camp, he was to leave Charbonneau and the Indian woman to hasten the return of the Indians with their horses to this place, and to proceed himself with the eleven men down the Columbia in order to examine the river; and, if he found it navigable and could obtain timber, to set about making canoes immediately. In the meantime, I was to bring on the party and baggage to the Shoshone camp, calculating that by the time I should reach that place, he would have sufficiently informed himself with respect to the state of the river, &c., to determine us whether to prosecute our journey from thence by land or water. . . .

Trading for Horses

[Lewis]   August 18th, 1805

This morning, while Captain Clark was busily engaged in preparing for his route, I exposed some articles to barter with the Indians for horses, as I wished a few at this moment to relieve the men who were going with Captain Clark from the labor of carrying their baggage, and also one to keep here in order to pack the meat to camp which the hunters might kill. I soon obtained three very good horses, for which I gave a uniform coat, a pair of leggings, a few handkerchiefs, three knives, and some other small articles, the whole of which did not cost more than about $20 in the United States. The Indians seemed quite as well pleased with their bargain as I was. The men also purchased one for an old checked shirt, a pair of old leggings, and a knife. . . .

[Lewis]   August 24th, 1805

As the Indians who were on their way down the Missouri had a number of spare horses with them, I thought it probable that I could obtain some of them and therefore desired the chief to speak to them and inform me whether they would trade. They gave no positive answer but requested to see the goods which I was willing to give in exchange. I now produced some battle axes which I had made at Fort Mandan, with which they were much pleased. Knives also seemed in great demand among them. I soon purchased three horses and a mule.

I had now nine horses and a mule, and two which I had hired made twelve. These I had loaded, and the Indian women took the balance of the baggage. I had given the interpreter some articles with which to purchase a horse for the woman, which he had obtained. At twelve o'clock we set out, and passed the river below the forks, directing our route toward the cove along the track formerly mentioned. Most of the horses were heavily laden, and it appears to me that it will require at least 25 horses to convey our baggage along such roads as I expect we shall be obliged to pass in the mountains, I had now the inexpressible satisfaction to find myself once more under way with all my baggage and party. . . .

[After finding a passage through the mountains, the expedition reached the Columbia River. On a cold, rainy day, they finally gained their ultimate goal—the Pacific Ocean.]

[Clark]   November 3rd, 1805

A mountain which we suppose to be Mt. Hood is S. 85° E., about 47 miles distant from the mouth of Quicksand River. This mountain is covered with snow and in the range of mountains which we have passed through and is of a conical form, but rugged. After taking dinner at the mouth of this river, we proceeded on.

[Clark]   November 4th, 1805

Several canoes of Indians from the village above came down, dressed for the purpose, as I supposed, of paying us a friendly visit. They had scarlet and blue blankets, sailor jackets, overalls, sh[...]
dress. The most of t[...]
sprung with quiver[...]
flasks to hold their [...]
ing and disagreeabl[...]
treated them with ev[...]

During the time w[...]
pipe tomahawk whic[...]
ately searched every[...]
nothing of my tomal[...]
hawk, one of those s[...]
one of our interprete[...]
root of a tree near the[...]
pleased with those f[...]
moved off on their ret[...]
canoes which had pas[...]

[Clark]

Encamped under a [...]
site to a rock situated [...]
feet high and 20 feet ir[...]
a place clear of the tide[...]
the only place we coul[...]
we laid our mats. Rain[...]
two Indians accompan[...]
were detected in stealir[...]
canoe, which got separa[...]
this evening from a lar[...]
board side, below the hi[...]
too wide to see either the[...]
on the larboard side.

Great joy in camp. We [...]
Pacific Ocean which we [...]
and the roaring or noise n[...]
rocky shores (as I suppos[...]

[Clark]

Captain Lewis branded [...]
marked my name, the day[...]
party all cut the first letters[...]

in the bottom[...]
ducks today.

In the eveni[...]
over in a canoe[...]
for which they[...]
that we were [...]
small stock of[...]
sistence on ou[...]
who had one [...]
kerchief, a bu[...]
coin, all of w[...]
shack, which [...]
but few of wh[...]

[Clark]

I marked n[...]
a large pine t[...]
Capt. Wi[...]

The squaw b[...]
marrow was [...]
grease or tall[...]
turned after [...]
greater part [...]
which they l[...]

[Clark]

We set ou[...]
pitched on fo[...]
and dined in[...]
ceeded on a[...]
miles to a h[...]
ment we pro[...]
is in the cen[...]

[Clark]

We havin[...]
lated for ou[...]
course as I [...]
and appeare[...]
pal object i[...]

or route that the men out hunting might find the direction to the fort if they should get lost in cloudy weather; and see the probability of game in that direction, for the support of the men we shall send to make salt.

[Clark]   9th December, 1805

I set out in a westerly direction, crossed 3 slashes, and arrived at a creek. Met 3 Indians loaded with fresh salmon. Those Indians made signs that they had a town on the seacoast at no great distance, and invited me to go to their town. They had a canoe hid in the creek; we crossed in this little canoe. After crossing, 2 of the Indians took the canoe on their shoulders and carried it across to the other creek, about ¼ of a mile. We crossed the 2nd creek and proceeded on to the mouth of the creek, which makes a great bend. Above the mouth of this creek, or to the south, are 3 houses and about 12 families of the Clatsop nation. We crossed to those houses.

Those people treated me with extraordinary friendship. One man attached himself to me as soon as I entered the hut, spread down new mats for me to sit on, gave me fish, berries, roots, etc. All the men of the other houses came and smoked with me. In the evening an old woman presented in a bowl made of a light-colored horn, a kind of syrup made of dried berries which the natives call *shele-well.* They gave me a kind of soup made of bread of the shele-well berries mixed with roots, which they presented in neat trenchers made of wood.

When I was disposed to go to sleep, the man who had been most attentive, named Cuscalah, produced 2 new mats and spread them near the fire, and directed his wife to go to his bed, which was the signal for all to retire. I had not been long on my mats before I was attacked most violently by the fleas, and they kept up a close siege during the night.

John C. Frémont Conquers the Rockies

John C. Frémont

John C. Frémont was one of the most famous explorers of the nineteenth century. With a team of mapmakers, scientists, soldiers and scout Kit Carson, he explored the Oregon Trail in 1842 and 1843. His lively accounts told of five great expeditions including his monumental climb of Frémont Peak in the Wyoming Rockies, crossing the Great Salt Lake in a raft, and fighting Indians in the Mohave Desert.

In this account from his journal of the first expedition, the great explorer chronicled his ascent of one of the tallest peaks of the Rockies. The expedition was almost out of food, and the ten-thousand-foot altitude was making Frémont and his men violently sick with headaches and vomiting. Frémont pushed on past undiscovered lakes and waterfalls, taking scientific measurements of position and altitude as he went along. After a breakfast of dried buffalo meat, Frémont scaled the highest peak and "unfurled the national flag to wave in the breeze where never flag waved before."

Frémont was one of the most important pathfinders to explore the west. His reports were published in eastern newspapers in New York and Boston. His lively adventures excited the nation and inspired many to move west. The accounts were so accurate, they were used by the pioneers as a trail guide to measure distances, locate campgrounds, fords, and mountain passes.

Excerpted from *The Pioneer West*, edited by Joseph Lewis French (Boston: Little, Brown and Company, 1923).

*A*ugust 10 [1842].—The air at sunrise is clear and pure, and the morning extremely cold, but beautiful. A lofty snow peak of the mountain is glittering in the first rays of the sun, which has not yet reached us. The long mountain wall to the east, rising two thousand feet abruptly from the plain, behind which we see the peaks, is still dark, and cuts clear against the glowing sky. A fog, just risen from the river, lies along the base of the mountain. A little before sunrise, the thermometer was at 35°, and at sunrise 33°. Water froze last night, and fires are very comfortable. The scenery becomes hourly more interesting and grand, and the view here is truly magnificent; but, indeed, it needs something to repay the long prairie journey of a thousand miles. The sun has just shot above the wall, and makes a magical change. The whole valley is glowing and bright, and all the mountain peaks are gleaming like silver. Though these snow mountains are not the Alps, they have their own character of grandeur and magnificence, and will doubtless find pens and pencils to do them justice. . . .

Provisions

Our animals had become very much worn out with the length of the journey; game was very scarce; and, though it does not appear in the course of the narrative (as I have avoided dwelling upon trifling incidents not connected with the objects of the expedition), the spirits of the men had been much exhausted by the hardships and privations to which they had been subjected. Our provisions had well-nigh all disappeared. Bread had been long out of the question; and of all our stock we had remaining two or three pounds of coffee and a small quantity of macaroni, which had been husbanded with great care for the mountain expedition we were about to undertake. Our daily meal consisted of dry buffalo meat cooked in tallow; and, as we had not dried this with Indian skill, part of it was spoiled, and what remained of good was as hard as wood, having much the taste and appearance of so many pieces of bark. Even of this, our stock was rapidly diminishing in a camp which was capable of consuming two buffaloes in every twenty-four hours. These animals had entirely disappeared, and it was not probable that we should fall in with them again until we returned to the Sweet Water.

Our arrangements for the ascent were rapidly completed. We were in a hostile country, which rendered the greatest vigilance and circumspection necessary. The pass at the north end of the mountain was generally infested by Black-feet; and immediately opposite was one of their forts, on the edge of a little thicket, two or three hundred feet from our encampment. We were posted in a grove of beech, on the margin of the lake, and a few hundred feet long, with a narrow *prairillon* on the inner side, bordered by the rocky ridge. In the upper end of this grove we cleared a circular space about forty feet in diameter, and with the felled timber and interwoven branches surrounded it with a breast-work five feet in height. A gap was left for a gate on the inner side, by which the animals were to be driven in and secured, while the men slept around the little work. It was half hidden by the foliage, and, garrisoned by twelve resolute men, would have set at defiance any band of savages which might chance to discover them in the interval of our absence. Fifteen of the best mules, with fourteen men, were selected for the mountain party. Our provisions consisted of dried meat for two days, with our little stock of coffee and some macaroni. In addition to the barometer and a thermometer I took with me a sextant and spy-glass, and we had, of course, our compasses. In charge of the camp I left Brenier, one of my most trustworthy men, who possessed the most determined courage. . . .

Road into the Rockies

August 12.—Early in the morning we left the camp, fifteen in number, well armed, of course, and mounted on our best mules. A pack animal carried our provisions, with a coffee-pot and kettle and three or four tin cups. Every man had a blanket strapped over his saddle, to serve for his bed, and the instruments were carried by turns on their backs. We entered directly on rough and rocky ground, and, just after crossing the ridge, had the good fortune to shoot an antelope. We heard the roar, and had a glimpse of a waterfall as we rode along; and, crossing in our way two fine streams, tributary to the Colorado, in about two hours' ride we reached the top of the first row or range of the mountains. Here, again, a view of the most romantic beauty met our eyes. It seemed as if, from the vast expanse of uninteresting prairie we had passed over, Nature had collected all her beauties together in one chosen place. We were overlooking a deep valley, which was entirely occupied by three lakes, and from the brink the surrounding ridges rose precipitously five hundred and a thousand feet, covered with the dark green of the balsam pine, relieved on the border of the lake with the light foliage of the aspen. They all communicated with each other; and the green of the waters, common to mountain lakes of great depth, showed that it would be impossible to cross them. The surprise manifested by our guides when these impassable obstacles suddenly barred our progress proved that they were among the hidden treasures of the place, unknown even to the wandering trappers of the region. . . .

While supper was being prepared, I set out on an excursion in the neighborhood, accompanied by one of my men. We wandered about among the crags and ravines until dark, richly repaid for our walk by a fine collection of plants, many of them in full bloom. Ascending a peak to find the place of our camp, we saw that the little defile in which we lay communicated with the long green valley of some stream, which, here locked up in the mountains, far away to the south, found its way in a dense forest to the plains.

Looking along its upward course, it seemed to conduct by a smooth gradual slope directly toward the peak, which, from long consultation as we approached the mountain, we had decided to be the highest of the range. Pleased with the discovery of so fine a road for the next day, we hastened down to the camp, where we arrived just in time for supper. Our table service was rather scant; and we held the meat in our hands, and clean rocks made good plates on which we spread our macaroni. Among all the strange places on which we had occasion to encamp during our long journey, none have left so vivid an impression on my mind as the camp of this evening. The disorder of the masses which surrounded us, the little hole through which we saw the stars overhead, the dark pines where we slept, and the rocks lit up with the glow of our fires made a night picture of very wild beauty.

August 13.—The morning was bright and pleasant, just cool enough to make exercise agreeable; and we soon entered the defile I had seen the preceding day. It was smoothly carpeted with a soft grass and scattered over with groups of flowers, of which yellow was the predominant color. Sometimes we were forced by an occasional difficult pass to pick our way on a narrow ledge along the side of the defile, and the mules were frequently on their knees; but these obstructions were rare, and we journeyed on in the sweet morning air, delighted at our good fortune in having found such a beautiful entrance to the mountains. . . .

Toward the Peak

I determined to leave our animals here and make the rest of our way on foot. The peak appeared so near that there was no doubt of our returning before night; and a few men were left in charge of the mules, with our provisions and blankets. We took with us nothing but our arms and instruments, and, as the day had become warm, the greater part left our coats. Having made an early dinner, we started again. We were soon involved in the most ragged precipices, nearing the central chain very slowly, and rising but little. The first ridge hid a succession of others; and when, with great fatigue and difficulty, we had climbed up five hundred feet, it was but to make an equal descent on the other side. All these intervening places were filled with small deep lakes, which met the eye in every direction, descending from one level to another, sometimes under bridges formed by huge fragments of granite, beneath which was heard the roar of the water. These constantly obstructed our path, forcing us to make long *détours*, frequently obliged to retrace our steps, and frequently falling among the rocks. Maxwell was precipitated toward the face of a precipice, and saved himself from going over by throwing himself flat on the ground. We clambered on, always expecting with every ridge that we crossed to reach the foot of the peaks, and always disappointed, until about four o'clock, when, pretty well worn out, we reached the shore of a little lake in which there was a rocky island. We remained here a short time to rest, and continued on around the lake, which had in some places a beach of white sand, and in others was bound with rocks, over which the way was difficult and dangerous, as the water from innumerable springs made them very slippery.

By the time we had reached the further side of the lake, we found ourselves all exceedingly fatigued, and, much to the satisfaction of the whole party, we encamped. . . .

Altitude Sickness

I was taken ill shortly after we had encamped, and continued so until late in the night, with violent headache and vomiting. This was probably caused by the excessive fatigue I had undergone and want of food, and perhaps also in some measure by the rarity of the air. The night was cold, as a violent gale from the north had sprung up at sunset, which entirely blew away the heat of the fires. The cold and our granite beds had not been favorable to sleep, and we were glad to see the face of the sun in the morning. Not being delayed by any preparation for breakfast, we set out immediately.

On every side as we advanced was heard the roar of waters and of a torrent, which we followed up a short distance until it expanded into a lake about one mile in length. On the northern side of the lake was a bank of ice, or rather of snow covered with a crust of ice. Carson had been our guide into the mountains, and agreeably to his advice we left this little valley and took to the ridges again, which we found extremely broken and where we were again involved among precipices. Here were ice fields; among which we were all dispersed, seeking each the best path to ascend the peak. Mr. Preuss attempted to walk along the upper edge of one of these fields, which sloped away at an angle of about twenty degrees; but his feet slipped from under him, and he went plunging down the plane. A few hundred feet below, at the bottom, were some fragments of sharp rock, on which he landed, and, though he turned a couple of somersets, fortunately received no injury beyond a few bruises. Two of the men, Clément Lambert and Descoteaux, had been taken ill, and lay down on the rocks a short distance below; and at this point I was attacked with headache and giddiness, accompanied by vomiting, as on the day before. . . .

Snow Peak

August 15.— . . . When we had secured strength for the day by a hearty breakfast, we covered what remained, which was enough for one meal, with rocks, in order that it might be safe from any marauding bird, and, saddling our mules, turned our faces once more towards the peaks. This time we determined to proceed quietly and cautiously, deliberately resolved to accomplish our object, if it were within the compass of human means. We were of opinion that a long defile which lay to the left of yesterday's route would lead us to the foot of the main peak. Our mules had been refreshed by the fine grass in the little ravine at the island camp, and we intended to ride up the defile as far as possible, in order to husband our strength for the main ascent. Though this was a fine passage, still it was a defile of the most rugged mountains known, and we had many a rough and steep slippery place to cross before reaching the end. In this place the sun rarely shone. Snow lay along the border of the small stream which flowed through it, and occasional icy passages made the footing of the mules very insecure; and the rocks and ground were moist with the trickling waters in this spring of mighty rivers. We soon had the satisfaction to find ourselves riding along the huge wall which forms the central summits of the chain. There at last it rose by our sides, a nearly perpendicular wall of granite, terminating 2,000 to 3,000 feet above our heads in a serrated line of broken, jagged cones. We rode on until we came almost immediately below the main peak, which I denominated the Snow Peak, as it exhibited more snow to the eye than any of the neighboring summits. Here were three small lakes of a green color, each of perhaps a thousand yards in diameter, and apparently very deep. These lay in a kind of chasm; and, according to the barometer, we had attained but a few hundred feet above the Island Lake. The barometer here stood at 20.450, attached thermometer 70°.

We managed to get our mules up to a little bench about a hundred feet above the lakes, where there was a patch of good grass, and turned them loose to graze. During our rough ride to this place, they had exhibited a wonderful surefootedness. Parts of the defile were filled with angular, sharp fragments of rock,—three or four and eight or ten feet cube,—and among these they had worked their way, leaping from one narrow point to another, rarely making a false step, and giving us no occasion to dismount. Having divested ourselves of every unnecessary encumbrance, we commenced the ascent. This time, like experienced travellers, we did not press ourselves, but climbed leisurely, sitting down as soon as we found breath beginning to fail. At intervals we reached places where a number of springs gushed from the rocks, and about 1,800 feet above the lakes came to the snow line. From this point our progress was uninterrupted climbing. Hitherto I had worn a pair of thick moccasins, with soles of *parflêche*; but here I put on a light thin pair, which I had brought for the purpose, as now the use of our toes became necessary to a further advance. I availed myself of a sort of comb of the mountain, which stood against the wall like a buttress, and which the wind and the solar radiation, joined to the steepness of the smooth rock, had kept almost entirely free from snow. Up this I made my way rapidly. Our cautious method of advancing in the outset had spared my strength; and, with the exception of a slight disposition to headache, I felt no remains of yesterday's illness. In a few minutes we reached a point where the buttress was overhanging, and there was no other way of surmounting the difficulty than by passing around one side of it, which was the face of a vertical precipice of several hundred feet.

Putting hands and feet in the crevices between the blocks, I succeeded in getting over it, and, when I reached the top, found my companions in a small valley below. Descending to them, we continued climbing, and in a short time reached the crest. I sprang upon the summit, and another step would have precipitated me into an immense snow field five hundred feet below. To the edge of this field was a sheer icy precipice; and then, with a gradual fall, the field sloped off for about a mile, until it struck the foot of another lower ridge. I stood on a narrow crest, about three feet in width, with an inclination of about 20° N. 51° E. As soon as I had gratified the first feelings of curiosity, I descended, and each man ascended in his turn; for I would only allow one at a time to mount the unstable and precarious slab, which it seemed a breath would hurl into the abyss below. We mounted the barometer in the snow of the summit, and, fixing a ramrod in a crevice, unfurled the national flag to wave in the breeze where never flag waved before.

The Discovery of Beckwourth Pass

James P. Beckwourth

James P. Beckwourth, an African American, worked for five
years as a blacksmith in St. Louis before he gave up his ham-
mer and tongs and became an expert with gun, bowie knife,
and tomahawk. He joined General William Ashley's Rocky
Mountain Company and explored the upper Missouri River
including Wyoming and Utah. It was with the Rocky Mountain Company that he earned a reputation as a master story-
teller who enjoyed spinning exaggerated tales with himself as
the hero. In 1828, he was captured and adopted by the Crow
Indians. He soon became war chief and fought in many battles
against the Blackfeet who were the Crow's enemy.

Beckwourth was always restless for new explorations, and
in 1850 made the discovery that was to earn his place in history. While prospecting in the mountains, he discovered an
important pass through the Sierra Nevada near present-day
Reno, Nevada. The pass was lower in elevation and much
safer for emigrants than the rugged and dangerous Donner
Trail. Beckwourth worked on the trail for a year and guided
the first wagon train of settlers through the pass. The trail was
used heavily by settlers traveling into California. He also set
up a hotel and store to supply the wagon trains going over the
pass. Today the pass, mountain peak, valley, and nearby town
all bear his name. He wrote an autobiography in 1892 to doc-
ument his achievements.

Excerpted from *The Life and Adventures of James P. Beckwourth*, edited by T.D. Bonner
(New York: Alfred A. Knopf, 1931).

We proceeded in an easterly direction, and all busied themselves in searching for gold; but my errand was of a different character; I had come to discover what I suspected to be a pass.

It was the latter end of April when we entered upon an extensive valley at the northwest extremity of the Sierra range. . . . Swarms of wild geese and ducks were swimming on the surface of the cool crystal stream, which was the central fork of the Rio de las Plumas [Feather River], or sailed the air in clouds over our heads. Deer and antelope filled the plains, and their boldness was conclusive that the hunter's rifle was to them unknown. Nowhere visible were any traces of the white man's approach, and it is probable that our steps were the first that ever marked the spot. We struck across this beautiful valley to the waters of the Yuba, from thence to the waters of the Truchy. . . . This, I at once saw, would afford the best waggon-road into the American Valley approaching from the eastward, and I imparted my views to three of my companions in whose judgment I placed the most confidence. They thought highly of the discovery, and even proposed to associate with me in opening the road. We also found gold, but not in sufficient quantity to warrant our working it. . . .

The Possibilities of Such a Road

On my return to the American Valley, I made known my discovery to a Mr. Turner, proprietor of the American Ranch, who entered enthusiastically into my views; it was a thing, he said, he had never dreamed of before. If I could but carry out my plan, and divert travel into that road, he thought I should be a made man for life. Thereupon he drew up a subscription-list, setting forth the merits of the project, and showing how the road could be made practicable to Bidwell's Bar, and thence to Marysville. . . . He headed the subscription with two hundred dollars.

When I reached Bidwell's Bar and unfolded my project, the town was seized with a perfect mania for the opening of the route. The subscriptions toward the fund required for its accomplishment amounted to five hundred dollars. . . . While thus busily engaged I was seized with erysipelas (a bacterial disease characterized by skin inflammation], and abandoned all hopes of recovery; I was over one hundred miles away from medical assistance, and my only shelter was a brush tent. I made my will, and resigned myself to death. Life still lingered in me, however, and a train of waggons came up, and encamped near where I lay. I was reduced to a very low condition, but I saw the drivers, and acquainted them with the object which had brought me out there. They offered to attempt the new road if I thought myself sufficiently strong to guide them through it. The women, God bless them! came to my assistance, and through their kind attentions and excellent nursing I rapidly recovered from my lingering sickness, until I was soon able to mount my horse, and lead the first train, consisting of seventeen waggons, through "Beckwourth's Pass." . . .

In the spring of 1852 I established myself in Beckwourth Valley, and finally found myself transformed into a hotel-keeper and chief of a trading-post. My house is considered the emigrant's landing-place, as it is the first ranch he arrives at in the golden state, and is the only house between this point and Salt Lake.

Chapter 2

Preparing for the Journey West

Chapter Preface

During the 1830s fur traders used wagons to haul their supplies and proved that the plains could be crossed by these four-wheeled vehicles. During the 1840s bad economic conditions, grasshopper plagues, free land granted by the Homestead Act, and the restless desire to travel to someplace new all played a part in the westward migration. The most common means of travel was the canvas-covered wagon known as the prairie schooner. The heavy-duty canvas top kept out the wind, rain, and dust. The large wooden wheels rolled over bumps and through potholes. The wagon's ten-foot-by-three-and-a-half-foot body could transport a ton and a half of weight. It was pulled by mules or oxen and could travel fifteen to twenty miles a day. A new wagon cost between sixty and ninety dollars and carried supplies that included food, spare parts, cooking utensils, guns, clothing, tools, and bedding. Some pioneers who could not afford wagons used mules, handcarts, or sometimes just walked.

The pioneers consulted guidebooks written by the pathfinders. The newspapers of the time were also filled with letters from settlers who had already made the journey. The timing of the trip was crucial. It was important to get to the jumping-off point on the Missouri River in April or May to start the journey in the spring. To reach the jumping-off point, pioneers from the East traveled by rail or steamboat. Independence, Missouri, was one of several towns along the Missouri River famous for equipping settlers for the trip. Once all of the supplies and animals were purchased, the last thing for the pioneers to do was to organize themselves. The members of the company elected a captain and formed governments to make decisions during the trip. Finally, once everything was ready, the wagons all assembled and the captain gave the signal to move out. The prairie schooners slowly moved onto the plains.

But all of the advice from experts and the careful preparations could not completely prepare them for the real hardships of the journey. Accidents, disease, hunger, and thirst were common on the trail. Often the only thing that kept the pioneers going was sheer determination.

The Prairie Traveler

Randolph B. Marcy

Captain Randolph B. Marcy wrote his pioneering guide at the request of the U.S. War Department in 1859. Marcy had twenty-five years experience exploring the west. Because of his great knowledge and his talent for writing, the book became the essential guide for settlers traveling west. It included information on what route to take, how to repair wagons, where to cross rivers, how to herd mules, when and how to trade with the Indians, and even a section on the dangers of quicksand. In this selection from his guide, Marcy tells how to organize a wagon train and elect a captain. He also describes the best type of wagons for the trip and the relative merits of using mules or oxen to pull them. He even explains how to pack for the trip and the best supplies for the journey. Marcy says he wrote this travel guide for the traveler "to avail himself of the matured experience of veteran travelers and thereby avoid many otherwise unforeseen disasters." Marcy's guide was a valuable tool that gave pioneers a good understanding of how to prepare for the trip and how to navigate the difficulties they would face along the way.

A fter a particular route has been selected to make the journey across the plains, and the requisite number have arrived at the eastern terminus, their first business should be to organize themselves into a company and elect a commander. The company should be of sufficient magnitude to herd and guard animals, and for protection against Indians.

From 50 to 70 men, properly armed and equipped, will

Excerpted from *The Prairie Traveler*, by Randolph B. Marcy (New York: Pedigree Books, 1859).

be enough for these purposes, and any greater number only makes the movements of the party more cumbersome and tardy.

In the selection of a captain, good judgment, integrity of purpose, and practical experience are the essential requisites, and these are indispensable to the harmony and consolidation of the association. His duty should be to direct the order of march, the time of starting and halting, to select the camps, detail and give orders to guards, and, indeed, to control and superintend all the movements of the company.

An obligation should then be drawn up and signed by all the members of the association, wherein each one should bind himself to abide in all cases by the orders and decisions of the captain, and to aid him by every means in his power in the execution of his duties; and they should also obligate themselves to aid each other, so as to make the individual interest of each member the common concern of the whole company. To ensure this, a fund should be raised for the purchase of extra animals to supply the places of those which may give out or die on the road; and if the wagon or team of a particular member should fail and have to be abandoned, the company should obligate themselves to transport his luggage, and the captain should see that he has his share of transportation equal with any other member. Thus it will be made the interest of every member of the company to watch over and protect the property of others as well as his own.

In case of failure on the part of anyone to comply with the obligations imposed by the articles of agreement after they have been duly executed, the company should of course have the power to punish the delinquent member, and, if necessary, to exclude him from all the benefits of the association. . . .

Wagons and Teams

A company having been organized, its first interest is to procure a proper outfit of transportation and supplies for the contemplated journey.

Wagons should be of the simplest possible construction—

strong, light, and made of well-seasoned timber, especially the wheels, as the atmosphere, in the elevated and arid region over which they have to pass, is so exceedingly dry during the summer months that, unless the woodwork is thoroughly seasoned, they will require constant repairs to prevent them from falling to pieces.

Wheels made of the bois-d'arc, or Osage orangewood, are the best for the plains, as they shrink but little, and seldom want repairing. As, however, this wood is not easily procured in the Northern States, white oak answers a very good purpose if well seasoned. . . .

There has been much discussion regarding the relative merits of mules and oxen for prairie traveling, and the question is yet far from being settled. Upon good firm roads, in a populated country, where grain can be procured, I should unquestionably give the preference to mules, as they travel faster, and endure the heat of summer much better than oxen; and if the journey be not over 1000 miles, and the grass abundant, even without grain, I think mules would be preferable. But when the march is to extend 1500 or 2000 miles, or over a rough, sandy or muddy road, I believe young oxen will endure better than mules; they will, if properly managed, keep in better condition, and perform the journey in an equally brief space of time. Besides, they are much more economical, a team of six mules costing six hundred dollars, while an eight-ox team only costs upon the frontier about two hundred dollars. Oxen are much less liable to be stampeded and driven off by Indians; and can be pursued and overtaken by horsemen; and, finally, they can, if necessary, be used for beef. . . .

Stores and Provisions

Supplies for a march should be put up in the most secure, compact, and portable shape.

Bacon should be packed in strong sacks of a hundred pounds to each; or, in very hot climates, put in boxes and surrounded with bran, which in a great measure prevents the fat from melting away.

If pork be used, in order to avoid transporting about forty percent of useless weight, it should be taken out of the barrels and packed like the bacon; then so placed in the bottom of the wagons as to keep it cool. The pork, if well cured, will keep several months in this way, but bacon is preferable.

Flour should be packed in stout double canvas sacks well sewed, a hundred pounds in each sack.

Butter may be preserved by boiling it thoroughly, and skimming off the scum as it rises to the top until it is quite clear like oil. It is then placed in tin canisters and soldered up. This mode of preserving butter has been adopted in the hot climate of southern Texas, and it is found to keep sweet for a great length of time, and its flavor is but little impaired by the process.

Sugar may be well secured in India rubber or gutta-percha sacks, or so placed in the wagon as not to risk getting wet.

Desiccated or dried vegetables are almost equal to the fresh, and are put up in such a compact and portable form as easily to be transported over the plains. They have been extensively used in the Crimean war, and by our own army in Utah, and have been very generally approved. They are prepared by cutting the fresh vegetables into thin slices and subjecting them to a very powerful press, which removes the juice and leaves a solid cake, which, after having been thoroughly dried in an oven, becomes almost as hard as a rock. A small piece of this, about half the size of a man's hand, when boiled, swells up so as to fill a vegetable dish, and is sufficient for four men. . . .

Only the Most Useful Articles

The allowance of provisions for each grown person, to make the journey from the Missouri River to California, should suffice for 110 days. The following is deemed requisite, viz.: 150 lbs. of flour, or its equivalent in hard bread; 25 lbs. of bacon or pork, and enough fresh beef to be driven on the hoof to make up the meat component of the ration; 15 lbs. of coffee, and 25 lbs. of sugar; also a quantity of saleratus or yeast powders for making bread, and salt and pepper.

These are the chief articles of subsistence necessary for the trip, and they should be used with economy, reserving a good portion for the western half of the journey. Heretofore many of the California emigrants have improvidently exhausted their stocks of provisions before reaching their journey's end, and have, in many cases, been obliged to pay the most exorbitant prices in making up the deficiency.

It is true that if persons choose to pass through Salt Lake City, and the Mormons happen to be in an amiable mood, supplies may sometimes be procured from them; but those who have visited them well know how little reliance is to be placed upon their hospitality or spirit of accommodation.

I once traveled with a party of New Yorkers en route for California. They were perfectly ignorant of everything relating to this kind of campaigning, and had overloaded their wagons with almost everything except the very articles most important and necessary; the consequence was that they exhausted their teams, and were obliged to throw away the greater part of their loading. They soon learned that Champagne, East India sweetmeats, olives, etc., etc., were not the most useful articles for a prairie tour.

Packing for the Trip to Oregon

Keturah Belknap

> Keturah Belknap used an ingenious method of keeping her
> diary. Beginning with her marriage on October 3, 1839, in
> Allen County, Ohio, she kept what she called "memorandum"
> in which she periodically recorded what had happened to her
> since her last written entry. Her "memorandum" are filled
> with vivid descriptions that give her story a lively, daily
> immediacy. In 1847, she and her husband, George, decided to
> follow others of the Belknap family out to Oregon. They
> would leave in the spring of 1848 and George's parents, Jesse
> and Jane Belknap, were to go with them.
>
> Belknap threw herself into the preparations for the trip. For
> months she worked day and night spinning thread, weaving
> cloth on a loom, and then hand sewing the thick linen wagon
> covers and clothing for the trip. She is a marvel of planning
> and industry right down to the last hour. She also managed to
> provide posterity with one of the best descriptions of these
> preparations that have been written. Belknap shows us the
> great self-reliance and energy with which the pioneers
> approached all their activities including getting ready for the
> journey west.

W e found the folks all excitement about Oregon. Some
had gone in the spring of '47; four families of the
connection and many of the neighbors but they had not been
heard from since crossing the Missouri River. Everything

Excerpted from diary entries dated 1847–1848, by Keturah Belknap, in *Covered Wagon
Women: Diaries & Letters from the Western Trails, 1840–1849, Vol. I*, edited by Kenneth
L. Holmes (Cleveland: A.H. Clark, 1983). Copyright © 1983 by Kenneth L. Holmes.
Reprinted with permission.

was out of place and all was excitement and commotion. . . .

There was nothing done or talked of but what had Oregon in it and the loom was banging and the wheel buzzing and trades being made from daylight till bed time. . . .

My dear little girl, Martha, was sick all summer and the 30th of October she died, one year and one month old. Now we have one little baby boy left.

So now I will spend what little strength I have left getting ready to cross the Rockies. Will cut out some sewing to have to pick up at all the odd moments for I will try to have clothes enough to last a year.

November 15, 1847. Have cut out four muslin shirts for George and two suits for the little boy (Jessie). With what he has that will last him (if he lives) until we will want a different pattern.

The material for the men's outer garments has to be woven yet. The neighbors are all very kind to come in to see me so I don't feel lonely like I would and they don't bring any work, but just pick up my sewing we think I will soon get a lot done. Then they are not the kind with long sad faces but always leave me with such a pleasant smiling faces that it does me good to think of them and I try not to think of the parting time but look forward to the time when we shall meet to part no more.

Preparing for the Trip

Now, I will begin to work and plan to make everything with an eye to starting out on a six month trip. The first thing is to lay plans and then work up to the program so the first thing is to make a piece of linen for a wagon cover and some sacks; will spin mostly evenings while my husband reads to me. The little wheel in the corner don't make any noise. I spin for Mother B. and Mrs. Hawley and they will weave; now that it is in the loom I must work almost day and night to get the filling ready to keep the loom busy. The men are busy making ox yokes and bows for the wagon covers and trading for oxen.

Now the New Year has come and I'll write (1848). This

is my program: will start out with the New Year. My health is better and I don't spend much time with house work. Will make a muslin cover for the wagon as we will have to double cover so we can keep warm and dry; put the muslin on first and then the heavy linen one for strength. They both have to be sewed real good and strong and I have to spin the thread and sew all these long seams with my fingers, then I have to make a new feather tick for my bed. I will put the feathers of two beds into one tick and sleep on it.

February 1st, and the linen is ready to work on and six two bushel bags all ready to sew up, that I will do evenings by the light of a dip candle for I have made enough to last all winter after we get to Oregon, and now my work is all planned so I can go right along. Have cut out two pairs of pants for George (Home made jeans). A kind lady friend came in today and sewed all day on one pair; then took them home with her to finish. Another came and wanted to buy some of my dishes and she took two shirts home to make to pay for them.

And now it is March and we have our team all ready and in good condition. Three good yoke of oxen and a good wagon. The company have arranged to start the 10th of April. I expect to load up the first wagon. George is practicing with the oxen. I dont want to leave my kind friends here but they all think it best so I am anxious to get off. I have worked almost day and night this winter, have the sewing about all done but a coat and vest for George. He got some nice material for a suit and had a taylor cut it out and Aunt Betsy Starr helped me two days with them so I am about ready to load up. Will wash and begin to pack and start with some old clothes on and when we can't wear them any longer will leave them on the road.

I think we are fixed very comfortable for the trip. There is quite a train of connection. Father Belknap has one wagon and 4 yoke of oxen; Hayley has two wagons and 8 yoke of oxen; Newton about the same; Uncle John Starr has two wagons and 4 yoke of oxen; G.W. Bethards one wagon and 3 yoke of oxen; we have the same besides 3 horses and 10 cows. Now it is the 1st of April and the stock is all in our corn field to get them used to running together; in ten days more we will be on the road.

Last Week at Home

This week I will wash and pack away everything except what we want to wear on the trip. April 5th. This week I cook up something to last us a few days till we get used to camp fare. Bake bread, make a lot of crackers and fry doughnuts, cook a chicken, boil ham, and stew some dryed fruit. There is enough to last us over the first Sunday so now we will begin to gather up the scatterings. Tomorrow is Saturday and next Tuesday we start so will put in some things today. Only one more Sunday here; some of the folks will walk to meeting. We have had our farewell meeting so I wont go; don't think I could stand it so George stays with me and we will take a rest for tomorrow will be a busy day.

Loading the Wagon

Monday, April 9th, 1848. I am the first one up; breakfast is over; our wagon is backed up to the steps; we will load at the hind end and shove the things in front. The first thing is a big box that will just fit in the wagon bed. That will have the bacon, salt and various other things; then it will be covered with a cover made of light boards nailed on two pieces of inch plank about 3 inches wide. This will serve us for a table, there is a hole in each corner and we have sticks sharpened at one end so they will stick in the ground; then we put the box cover on, slip the legs in the holes and we have a nice table, then when it is on the box George will sit on it and let his feet hang over and drive the team. It is just as high as the wagon bed. Now we will put in the old chest that is packed with our clothes and things we will want to wear and use on the way. The till is the medicine chest; then there will be cleats fastened to the bottom of the wagon bed to keep things from slipping out of place. Now there is a vacant place clear across that will be large enough to set a chair; will set it with the back against the side of wagon bed;

there I will ride. On the other side will be a vacancy where little Jessie can play. He has a few toys and some marbles and some sticks for whip stocks, some blocks for oxen and I tie a string on the stick and he uses my work basket for a covered wagon and plays going to Oregon. He never seems to get tired or cross. . . . The next thing is a box as high as the chest that is packed with a few dishes and things we wont need till we get thru. And now we will put in the long sacks of flour and other things. The sacks are made of home made linen and will hold 125 pounds; 4 sacks of flour and one of corn meal. Now comes the groceries. We will make a wall of smaller sacks stood on end; dried apples and peaches, beans, rice, sugar and coffee, the latter being in the green state. We will brown it in a skillet as we want to use it. Everything must be put in strong bags; no paper wrappings for the trip. There is a corner left for the wash-tub and the lunch basket will just fit in the tub. The dishes we want to use will all be in the basket. I am going to start with good earthen dishes and if they get broken have tin ones to take their place. Have made 4 nice little table cloths so am going to live just like I was at home. Now we will fill the other corner with pick-ups. The iron-ware that I will want to use every day will go in a box on the hind end of the wagon like a feed box. Now we are loaded all but the bed. I wanted to put it in and sleep out but George said I wouldn't rest any so I will level up the sacks with some extra bedding, then there is a side of sole leather that will go on first, then two comforts and we have a good enough bed for anyone to sleep on. At night I will turn my chair down and make the bed a little longer so now all we will have to do in the morning is put in the bed and make some coffee and roll out.

All Is Ready

The wagon looks so nice, the nice white cover drawn down tight to the side boards with a good ridge to keep from sagging. It's high enough for me to stand straight under the roof with a curtain to put down in front and one at the back end. Now it is all done and I get in out of the tumult. And now everything is ready I will rest a little, then we will eat a bite. Mother B. has made a pot of mush and we are all going to eat mush and milk to save the milk that otherwise would have to be thrown out. Then we have prayers and then to bed.

Tuesday, April 10, 1848. Daylight dawned with none awake but me. I try to keep quiet so as not to wake anyone but pretty soon Father Belknap's voice was heard with that well-known sound "Wife, Wife, rise and flutter" and there was no more quiet for anyone. Breakfast is soon over; my dishes and food for lunch is packed away and put in its proper place, the iron things are packed in some old pieces of old thick rags. Now for the bed (feather); nicely folded the two ends together, lay it on the sacks, then I fix it. The covers are folded and the pillows laid smoothly on, reserving one for the outside so if I or the little boy get sleepy we have a good place to lie; the others are covered with a heavy blanket and now my chair and the churn and we will be all done.

Our wagon is ready to start.

Saying Good-Bye to Friends and Family

Phoebe Goodell Judson

Phoebe Goodell Judson was twenty when she set out on her journey to Washington Territory in 1853. Her parents had already immigrated to the Willamette Valley in Oregon. Phoebe had married Holden Judson three years earlier. They were determined to take advantage of the government's offer of free land and to endure whatever hardships they might encounter, "in order to secure a home that we might call 'ours.'" And so Phoebe and Holden said good-bye to her childhood home of Vermillion, Ohio, on the civilized shore of Lake Erie. They set off, "dreaming our future lives were destined to be passed together on the far away shore of Puget Sound." It would take them six months of hard traveling across prairies, rivers, deserts, and mountains before they could even begin to realize their dream. She wrote this memoir when she was ninety-five and intended it to be a record of the "homely, everyday incidents of a plain woman."

Our pioneer story begins where love stories (more is the pity) frequently terminate, for Holden Allen Judson and Phoebe Newton Goodell had been joined in the holy bonds of matrimony three years before we decided to emigrate to the vast and uncultivated wilderness of Puget Sound, which at that time was a part of Oregon.

Little did I realize how much it meant when I promised the solemn, but kindly faced, minister in the presence of a

Excerpted from *A Pioneer's Search for an Ideal Home*, by Phoebe Goodell Judson (Lincoln: University of Nebraska Press, 1984).

large assembly of friends, to obey, as well as to love, the one whom I had chosen for a partner through life, for the thought of becoming a pioneer's wife had never entered my mind; but it is not surprising that a girl of only seventeen summers, romantically inclined, should have chosen from among her suitors one possessing a spirit of adventure.

Mr. Judson was five years my senior. Seldom were two more congenially mated to travel the rough voyage of life. Both were endowed with vigorous health, fired with ambition and a love of nature.

Our childhood days were spent together in the little town of Vermillion, Ohio, located midway between Cleveland and Sandusky, on the shores of Lake Erie, on whose beaches we strolled, and on whose blue waters we sailed in company, little dreaming our future lives were destined to be passed together on the far away shore of Puget Sound. . . .

Dream Home

The motive that induced us to part with pleasant associations and the dear friends of our childhood days, was to obtain from the government of the United States a grant of land that "Uncle Sam" had promised to give to the head of each family who settled in this new country. This, we hoped, would make us independent, for as yet we did not possess a home of our own—all of which meant so much to us that we were willing to encounter dangers, endure hardships and privations in order to secure a home that we might call "ours."

The many air castles that I built concerning my "ideal home" while the preparations for our long journey were being made, are still fresh in my memory.

It should be built by a mountain stream that flowed to the Pacific, or by some lake, or bay, and nothing should obstruct our view of the beautiful snow-capped mountains.

True, it would be built of logs, but they would be covered with vines and roses, while the path leading to it should be bordered with flowers and the air filled with their sweet perfume.

"Home, home, sweet home;
Be it ever so humble,
There's no place like home."

My parents had already found a home on the banks of the
Willamette, in Oregon.

Good-Byes

The parting with my husband's parents and only sister was
very affecting, as he was their only son and brother, and our
little two-year-old Annie their idol.

The time set for our departure was March 1st, 1853.
Many dear friends gathered to see us off. The tender "good-
byes" were said with brave cheers in the voices, but many
tears from the hearts. After we were seated in the stage that
was to carry us forth on the first part of our journey into the
"wide, wide world," little Annie put out her hands and asked
"Fazzer," as she called her grandpapa, to take her. He
begged us to leave her with them—mother and Lucretia sec-
onding his request with tearful eyes. Her sweet young life
was interwoven with theirs, and well I knew the anguish that
rent their hearts at the parting with their little darling.
Deeply we sympathized with them in their grief, but how
could we part with our only treasure?

Amid the waving of handkerchiefs and the lingering
"God bless you" the stage rolled away—and we were embarked on our long and perilous journey.

Our route lay along the lake shore road as we journeyed, and as the distance increased between our loved
ones—father, mother, sister and the dear home environ-
ments, my heart grew heavy. I realized we were for the last
time gazing upon the waters of beautiful Lake Erie, upon
whose sandy beaches I, with my twin sister, had whiled
away many, many happy hours gathering the little periwin-
kles and other shells, or rowing upon its placid waters; never
tiring of watching the steamers and other vessels sail into
the harbor, or hastening to the islands of Put In Bay for protection in time of storm. . . .

My mind was occupied with many sad reflections until

we reached Sandusky City, where we boarded the train for Cincinnati. 'Twas here we parted with my dear brother, William, who had accompanied us this far on our journey. From my car window I saw he was weeping, while I could scarcely refrain from sobbing aloud. He was but two years my senior, and we were both much attached to each other. He was married a few days before our departure, that we might attend his wedding, and with his young wife emigrated to this coast the following year.

Riding on the train was a new experience for me—the interest and novelty of the trip served in a measure to alleviate the sadness of parting. It was before the day of fast trains, and, though owing to my inexperience, we seemed to be moving very rapidly, the trip consumed the entire day; and it was long after dusk when we reached Cincinnati. The depot was some distance from our hotel and the deafening rattle of the cab wheels over the cobble stones frightened little Annie, and she cried piteously to be carried back home.

The hotel accommodations were luxurious. As we rested in the pleasant parlor a short time before retiring to our rooms, a lady played the piano and sang that pathetic song, "The Old Folks at Home."

The sentiment of the sweet old song harmonized with my feelings and caused the tears to flow afresh, as I thought of the dear father and mother we had left in their lonely home. The music soothed Annie's fears. She sat in my lap and talked about poor "Fazzer, mozzer and Aunt Trecia," as she called them, until she fell asleep.

Steamer to St. Louis

In the morning we boarded a steamer. I have forgotten her name, but she was a floating palace for those days, and was loaded with passengers bound for the "far west."

We steamed rapidly down the Ohio and up the Mississippi. The pleasure of this voyage would have been without alloy, but the third day little Annie was taken very ill, and for a time we were much alarmed; but with simple remedies and good nursing she recovered without the aid of a physician.

The deafening whanging and banging of the gong startled us from our slumbers in the morning, calling us to a bountifully spread table. We greatly enjoyed the luxurious meals with which we were served on these river boats.

To while away the time, many of the passengers indulged in dancing and simple games of cards, which seemed innocent amusements; but after awhile, to my horror, I learned that others were gambling—risking their fortunes, many times beggaring their innocent families by a single throw of the dice. Although there were no bloody affrays on the boat, still I knew that gambling frequently led to murders, and the iniquity of this awful practice filled my soul with terror and I was in constant dread that the vengeance of an angry God would be visited upon us, by the blowing up, or sinking, of the boat, with all on board. My religious training had taught me fear, instead of trust. My heart was filled with thankfulness when we reached St. Louis in safety, where we remained but one day and night.

Down the Missouri

Transferring our baggage to the little steamer "Kansas," we began the ascent of the Missouri river, which we found was a very difficult and dangerous stream to navigate. Only light draft steamers were able to stem the current of its turbulent waters and make their way around the many jams and snags with which it was obstructed, and over the logs which made the little steamer bend and creak as though she was breaking in two. Our progress was slow and we were ten long days in reaching our destination, feeling greatly relieved when we disembarked at what was then called "Kansas Landing," where now stands the large and flourishing city of Kansas City.

A number of our fellow travelers, who were emigrating to California and Oregon, went on to Council Bluff to purchase their "outfit" for the journey over the plains. They urged us to go on with them, which would have pleased us well, for they were enterprising and intelligent people, with congenial qualities, well fitting them for good citizens in a new country. But we were only too glad to leave the muddy Missouri.

We had made our arrangements, before leaving home, to purchase our outfit for our journey at this place, which seems quite providential, for the news came to us here that the steamer Kansas struck a snag and sank before reaching her destination—the unfortunate emigrants losing all of their baggage.

We were thankful to get this far without accident, not knowing what lay before us. We little realized this was a pleasure trip in comparison with the journey across the plains.

Outfitting for the Road to Virginia City

James Knox Polk Miller

By the time James Knox Polk Miller began his journey west at the age of nineteen, he had already experienced a lot of the world, even though he had never set foot outside his home state of New York. Orphaned at an early age, James went into business with his guardian and uncle in Clyde, New York. He ran away when a bad argument erupted between them. James left town taking part of the money from the business and leaving behind a large debt.

He began his diary when he arrived in Chicago in 1864. From Chicago he traveled by rail to the river town of St. Joseph, Missouri. St. Joseph was a jumping-off point. It was one of the towns on the Missouri River where pioneers came to be outfitted for the journey west. Miller and two fellow travelers spent several days buying horses, guns, wagons, supplies, and even a dog. They loaded up their wagon, crossed the Missouri on a ferry, and set out in a heavy rain on the road to Virginia City, Montana.

This account from Miller's book, *The Road to Virginia City*, shows him to be a practical and resourceful young man who is looking for a fresh start and new opportunities. He eventually found both. Miller traveled in the west for several years before settling down in Deadwood, South Dakota. There he became one of the most successful pioneer builders of the town and became the president of the Deadwood Central Railroad whose tracks supplied the very rich Homestead Mine.

Excerpted from *The Road to Virginia City*, by James Knox Polk Miller, edited by Andrew F. Rolle (Norman: University of Oklahoma Press, 1960). Copyright © 1960 by the University of Oklahoma Press. Reprinted with permission.

August 13, 1864. . . . Met my two friends of the day before. St. Joseph is a city of about 10,000 inhabitants slightly tainted with Secession, quite pleasantly situated upon the Missouri River, its chief business seems to be in providing mules, horses, wagons, provisions etc. for Emigrants & for the western mines etc. There are two good hotels, one of them now used as a military headquarters (Patee House) and it is a sort of military beehive. Found the sleepy baggage man had delivered my trunk to Pacific Hotel & I decided in consequence to change my quarters to the Pacific. My two friends and myself spent the day in examining some 100 head of stock, trying to select a span of horses & a saddle horse. I concluded finally to select a fine pacing horse "Frank." . . . After considerable talk my friends left me, agreeing to meet me at the Pacific at 7 o'clock and to report exactly what determination they had regarding our proposed way of traveling to the Pacific States. At about eight o'clock they arrived and to my great vexation postponed the time to eight o'clock tomorrow. Very hot and dusty. Telegraphic report last night from Atchison that owing to depredations and murders committed by the Indians thin stock at the stations had been called in & no stage would start before 10 days from today.

Outfitted for the Journey

August 14, 1864. Up at 7 o'clock, lounged about the Hotel reading [a novel of the Civil War] "Shoulder Straps" by Henry Morford awaiting the arrival of my two friends. At about 10 o'clock they arrived and we entered into the following arrangement. They are to put in $325 towards getting up an outfit to cross the plains and I am to furnish the balance of about $425. I to pay them .40¢ per lb. for my baggage over 25 lbs., that is their share of it as 325 is to 425. Found their names to be Geo. W. Brown & Edward Rushlow & from Rochester, N.Y. Upon concluding an arrangement we purchased a span of Bay horses for $400, Harness $35, and I purchased a fine saddle horse as before concluded, $200, looked at some wagons, made some purchases & returning to the Hotel. After supper I strolled to the river bank and returning to the Hotel retired after perusing "Shoulder Straps" awhile.

August 15, 1864. Was taken very sick during the night. Vomited very freely & had a very bad attack of Diahearea. At same time suffered a great deal of pain and did not get a moment's sleep. In morning was unable to leave my bed. Brown came up about eight o'clock, gave him $200 to purchase my saddle horse & $120 to pay on horses, he afterwards returning $10. Got downstairs about 10 o'clock very weak and without appetite, eating neither breakfast or dinner. In afternoon went to gun store & purchased three Wesson rifles, a Bowie knife, & 1000 Cartridges, I buying two of the Rifles and Rushlow one. Had to obtain Permit from the Provost before we could buy the Rifles. Obtained permit without trouble, the man belonging or having once lived at Albany. Purchased $139 worth of groceries, provisions etc., & gave $35 for wagon cover, cook stove etc. Loaded provisions into wagon so as to get an early start on the morrow. Returned to the Hotel, ate a piece of toast & drank a cup of tea after which 4 games of Billiards and I retired to Room No. 20.

First Day on the Trail

August 16, 1864. Up at 5½ o'clock. Dreary drizzly rain. Purchased a dog for $3 & various merchandise needed in our trip after getting all of which, including the dog, into the wagon paid my hotel bill, a very moderate one of $9. We proceeded to the ferry crossing the Missouri River nearly rolling into the river, owing to the steep bank upon which twenty four hours of steady rain had put a coat of mud about a foot thick which, affording a very precarious footing for the horses, made crossing with a load as heavy as ours very disagreeable. It was now raining quite freely. Brown in anything but a Dry humor preferring to ride horseback to riding in our "calaboose" succeeded in getting quite damp, especially his "nether" garments, his body being protected only by an oil cloth blanket. Traveled through a fine country, fields and woods having their best dress on owing to the rain. Arriving at Walthena a small town the chief points of interest being the well where we procured water for our horses, and a grocery store where we purchased a faucet for our Molasses Keg. I here mounted my pacer, the rain having ceased, & rode untill nightfall when we selected a roadside spot for our encampment covered with bushes three to four feet high & slightly sloping. Unhitching our team and riding them to water 200 yds. distant rode for the first time with only the Halter to guide by. Passing the halter through his mouth so as to form a bit it made an excellent bridle. After watering our horses we proceeded to a clump of trees a short distance off, & selecting a walnut stump, chipped off enough wood with our axe to last us, and taking our camp stove (made of sheet iron) we started a fire, Making some coffee to which of necessity we could not add milk though we carried best quality lump sugar. Cutting some dried beef & adding some hard tack we had supper after which we cleaned the horses, tied them to lariats & divided ourselves into watches, mine being from 2 to 4½ o'clock in the morning. I laid down upon my blankets to sleep. I found it very much impossible however. The circumstances & sensations were so new to me that I could only succeed in tiring myself out trying to sleep. The chirping of the Cricket so incessant and loud, the stomping & knawing of the horses tied to our wagon, in which upon our blankets we were trying to sleep, added to our danger from Guerellas & Indians— everyone we met reporting large bands & horrible murders & massacres only 200 miles from our Encampment, causing us to keep open our rifles—made such a new sensation that I arose having remained awake the entire night. During the day we passed a Tobacco field growing finely. Also a few stalks of hemp, the first of each I had ever seen.

Ham, Coffee, & Hard Tack

August 17, 1864. Our party up at 4½ o'clock. I was called in time for breakfast having had an hour's sleep. Made our breakfast of ham, coffee, & hard tack after which we greased our wagon & started. Country very beautifull. Too many hills to be called "Rolling" Plain but resembling very much. We reached Troy, the county seat of Dennison County, Kansas, a village of perhaps 200 inhabitants. Here we were again regaled with stories of the attacks of the Indians by a Pale faced specimen of humanity, a Dr[agoon] who was chiefly remarkable for having small feet & boots well blacked and being one of the Militia, the last as p[e]r his repeated statement. Passing along our route lay through what I think to be as fine a country as any in the world. Passing immense rolling Prairies on every side reaching as far as the eye can reach, with small clumps of trees from three to four miles apart, passing small farm houses, surrounded by large fields of corn. The country seems entirely destitute of fruit, watermelon being the only obtainable luxury and even Potatoes are almost unknown. After indefatigable efforts to obtain a Pie of some kind we were forced to the conclusion that they were as scarce as the Potatoes. Prairie chickens, quails, Pigeons very thick. Camped about 85 miles from St. Joe in front of a farm house. Water scarce. Hard work to get wood. Supper oyster stew (poor), beef, ham & coffee. My watch until 12 o'clock.

Almost Turning Back

Catherine Haun

Catherine Haun was a young bride when she and her husband decided to cross the plains in a prairie schooner. They wanted to leave behind some old debts and the cold winters of Iowa that were affecting Catherine's health and find a better life in California. In her reminiscence, dictated to her daughter many years after the 1849 journey, Haun vividly describes the details of furnishing the wagon for the trip. She tells about the clothing, food, medicine, and supplies they packed into their wagon. She also relates how a code of regulations was drawn up, officers elected and duties assigned to each member of the party once the wagons were assembled in a caravan. Despite their thorough preparations, Catherine and her husband had second thoughts after the first night on the trail. They were on the verge of turning back especially when the cook quit and left for home. To her surprise, Catherine volunteered to do the cooking despite the fact that she did not even know how to make a cup of coffee. In true pioneer spirit, Catherine quickly learned to make pancakes and the next day they continued their journey to California.

Early in January of 1849 we first thought of emigrating to California. . . .

Our discontent and restlessness were enhanced by the fact that my health was not good. Fear of my sister's having died while young of consumption, I had reason to be apprehensive on that score. The physician advised an entire change of climate thus to avoid the intense cold of Iowa, and recommended a sea voyage, but finally approved of our con-

Excerpted from "Diary of Mrs. Catherine Haun," by Catherine Haun, in *Women's Diaries of the Westward Journey*, edited by Lillian Schlissel (New York: Schocken Books, 1982).

templated trip across the plains in a "prairie schooner," for even in those days an out-of-door life was advocated as a cure for this disease. In any case, as in that of many others, my health was restored long before the end of our journey.

Full of the energy and enthusiasm of youth, the prospects of so hazardous an undertaking had no terror for us, indeed, as we had been married but a few months, it appealed to us as a romantic wedding tour.

The territory bordering upon the Mississippi River was, in those days, called "the west" and its people were accustomed to the privations and hardships of frontier life. It was mostly from their ranks that were formed the many companies of emigrants who traveled across the plains, while those who came to California from the Eastern states usually chose the less strenuous ocean voyage by way of the Isthmas of Panama or around the Horn. . . .

On the streets, in the fields, in the workshops and by the fireside, golden California was the chief topic of conversation. Who were going? How was best to "fix up" the "outfit"? What to take as food and clothing? Who would stay at home to care for the farm and womenfolks? Who would take wives and children along? Advice was handed out quite free of charge and often quite free of common sense. However, as two heads are better than one, all proffered ideas helped as a means to the end. The intended adventurers diligently collected their belongings and after exchanging such articles as were not needed for others more suitable for the trip, begging, buying or borrowing what they could, with buoyant spirits started off.

Some half dozen families of our neighborhood joined us and probably about twenty-five persons constituted our little band.

Fitting Out the Party

Our own party consisted of six men and two women. Mr. Haun, my brother Derrick, Mr. Bowen, three young men to act as drivers, a woman cook and myself. Mr. Haun was chosen Major of the company, and as was the custom in those days, his fellow travelers ever afterwards knew him by this title. Derrick was to look after the packing and unpacking coincident to camping at night, keep tab on the commissary department and, when occasion demanded, lend a "helping hand." The latter service was expected of us all— men and women alike, was very indefinite and might mean anything from building campfires and washing dishes to fighting Indians, holding back a loaded wagon on a downgrade or lifting it over bowlders when climbing a mountain.

Mr. Bowen furnished his own saddle horse, and for his services was brought free of expense to himself. His business was to provide the wood or fuel for the campfire, hunt wild game and ride ahead with other horsemen to select a camping ground or in search of water. He proved himself invaluable and much of the time we had either buffalo, antelope or deer meat, wild turkey, rabbits, prairie chickens, grouse, fish or small birds.

Eight strong oxen and four of the best horses on the farm were selected to draw our four wagons—two of the horses were for the saddle.

Two wagons were filled with merchandise which we hoped to sell at fabulous prices when we should arrive in the "land of gold." The theory of this was good but the practice—well, we never got the goods across the first mountain. Flour ground at our own grist mill and bacon of home-curing filled the large, four-ox wagon while another was loaded with barrels of alcohol. The third wagon contained our household effects and provisions. The former consisted of cooking utensils, two boards nailed together, which was to serve as our dining table, some bedding and a small tent. We had a very generous supply of provisions. All meats were either dried or salted, and vegetables and fruit were dried, as canned goods were not common sixty years or more ago. For luxuries we carried a gallon each of wild plum and crabapple preserves and blackberry jam. Our groceries were wrapped in India rubber covers and we did not lose any of them—in fact still had some when we reached Sacramento.

The two-horse spring wagon was our bed-room and was

driven by the Major—on good stretches of road by myself. A hair mattress, topped off with one of feathers and layed on the floor of the wagon with plenty of bedding made a very comfortable bed after a hard day's travel.

In this wagon we had our trunk of wearing apparel, which consisted of underclothing, a couple of blue checked gingham dresses, several large stout aprons for general wear, one light colored for Sundays, a pink calico sunbonnet and a white one intended for "dress up" days. . . .

Have All Things Ready to Start for Oregon by April

William J. Martin's advice to prospective pioneers appeared in the St. Joseph Gazette *in Platte City, Missouri, on January 23, 1846. Martin had traveled to Oregon in 1843 as a commander of a wagon train, and in 1846 was to lead another party along the Oregon Trail. His letter to the editor gives a good short list of everything a pioneer might need for the journey west. He urges, like a loud commercial spokesman, that crossing the Missouri River at St. Joseph "is by far the best route." Martin insists that all emigrants must have everything ready to depart by the tenth of April in order to reach Oregon by the fall and have time to build their cabins before the onset of winter.*

For the benefit of those who intend to emigrate in the spring, I beg the use of your columns for a few suggestions which they will find useful and important. I give them as briefly as possible, and without regard to style—matter is of more moment to such as wish to embark in this long trip.

First, the wagons should be sufficiently strong to carry from 2000 to 2500 lbs—they should be made with falling tongues.

Each wagon to have good double covers.

Each wagon to have at least three good yoke of oxen from 4 to 7 years old—the oxen should be well broken—yokes and bows to be all good and complete.

Two hundred pounds of flour to each person over ten years old—100 pounds to each child over three and under ten.

Across Iowa

When we started from Iowa I wore a dark woolen dress which served me almost constantly during the whole trip. Never without an apron and a three-cornered kerchief, similar to those worn in those days I presented a comfortable, neat appearance. The wool protected me from the sun's rays and penetrating prairie winds. Besides it economized in laundrying which was a matter of no small importance when one considers how limited, and often utterly wanting were

Fifteen pounds of coffee, and the same of sugar to each person.

100 pounds of bacon to each person over ten years old—

50 pounds to all over three and under ten.

50 pounds of salt to each mess.

50 pounds of rice to each mess.

5 pounds of pepper to each mess.

50 pounds of dried fruit, apples and peaches.

Each mess to have a good tent of sufficient size to contain from five to eight persons.

Each man to be armed with a good rifle or heavy shot gun, with 5 pounds of powder and twelve pounds of lead or fifteen pounds of shot to each man.

Emigrants should have all things completed and in readiness to start by the 10th of April at farthest. A great deal depends on starting early in the spring, so as to reach Oregon early in the fall, and have time to erect cabins for the winter, and put in wheat crops in time to be able to raise their own bread stuffs.

I would advise all persons who intend emigrating to Oregon from the Platte purchase or elsewhere, to cross the Missouri river AT ST. JOSEPH, AS THAT IS BY FAR THE BEST ROUTE.

Let me repeat and urge it upon all who intend emigrating in the spring, to have all things ready to start from the west bank of the Missouri by the 10th of April.

Dale Morgan, ed., *Overland in 1846: Diaries and Letters of the California-Oregon Trail.* Lincoln: University of Nebraska Press, 1993.

our "wash day" conveniences. The chief requisite, water, being sometimes brought from miles away.

In the trunk were also a few treasures; a bible, medicines, such as quinine, bluemass [a quinine derivative], opium, whiskey and hartshorn for snake bites and citric acid—an antidote for scurvey. A little of the acid mixed with sugar and water and a few drops of essence of lemon made a fine substitute for lemonade. Our matches, in a large-mouthed bottle were carefully guarded in this trunk.

The pockets of the canvas walls of the wagon held every day needs and toilet articles, as well as small fire arms. The ready shotgun was suspended from the hickory bows of the wagon camp. A ball of twine, an awl and buckskin strings for mending harness, shoes etc. were invaluable. It was more than three months before we were thoroughly equipped and on April 24th, 1849 we left our comparatively comfortable homes—and the uncomfortable creditors—for the uncertain and dangerous trip. . . .

There was still snow upon the ground and the roads were bad, but in our eagerness to be off we ventured forth. This was a mistake as had we delayed for a couple of weeks the weather would have been more settled, the roads better and much of the discouragement and hardship of the first days of travel might have been avoided.

Owing partly to the new order of things and partly to the saturated soil, travel was slow for our heavy laden wagons and untried animals. We covered only ten miles the first day and both man and beast were greatly fatigued. As I look back now it seems the most tiresome day of the entire trip.

That night we stopped at a farm and I slept in the farm house. When I woke the next morning a strange feeling of fear at the thought of our venturesome undertaking crept over me. I was almost dazed with dread. I hurried out into the yard to be cheered by the bright sunshine, but old Sol's very brightness lent such a glamor to the peaceful, happy, restful home that my faint heartedness was only intensified. . . . It was a restful scene—a contrast to our previous day of toil and discomfort and caused me to break completely down with genuine homesickness and I burst out into a flood of tears. . . . I remember particularly a flock of domesticated wild geese. They craned their necks at me and seemed to encourage me to "take to the woods." Thus construing their senseless clatter I paused in my grief to recall the intense cold of the previous winter and the reputed perpetual sunshine and wealth of the promised land. Then wiping away my tears, lest they betray me to my husband, I prepared to continue my trip. I have often thought that had I confided in him he would certainly have turned back, for he, as well as the other men of the party, was disheartened and was struggling not to betray it. . . .

In the morning our first domestic annoyance occurred. The woman cook refused point blank to go any further. Evidently she had not been encouraged by any wild geese for she allowed her tears to be seen and furthermore her Romeo had followed her and it did not require much pursuading on his part to induce her to return. Here was a dilemma! Had this episode happened on the previous morning when my stock of courage was so low and the men were all so busy with their own thoughts—our trip would have ended there.

Our first impulse was that we should have to return, but after a day's delay during [which] our disappointment knew no bounds, I surprised all by proposing to do the cooking, if everybody else would help. My self-reliance and the encouragement of our fellow travelers won the day and our party kept on. Having been reared in a slave state my culinary education had been neglected and I had yet to make my first cup of coffee. My offer was, however, accepted, and as quantity rather than quality was the chief requisite to satisfy our good appetites I got along very well, even though I never became an expert at turning pancakes (slap-jacks) by tossing them into the air. . . .

At the end of a month we reached Council Bluffs, having only travelled across the state of Iowa, a distance of about 350 miles every mile of which was beautifully green and well watered. We also had the advantage of camping near farm-houses and the generous supply of bread, butter, eggs and poultry greatly facilitated the cooking. Eggs were 2½ cents a dozen—at our journey's end we paid $1 a piece, that is when we had the dollar. Chickens were worth eight and ten cents a piece. When we reached Sacramento $10 was the ruling price and few to be had at that.

As Council Bluffs was the last settlement on the route we made ready for the final plunge into the wilderness by looking over our wagons and disposing of whatever we could spare. . . .

For the common good each party was "sized up" as it were. People insufficiently provisioned or not supplied with guns and ammunition were not desirable but, on the other hand, wagons too heavily loaded might be a hindrance. Such luxuries as rocking chairs mirrors, washstands and corner what-nots were generally frowned down upon and when their owners insisted upon carrying them they had to be abandoned before long on the roadside and were appropriated by the Indians who were always eager to get anything that might be discarded.

The canvas covered schooners were supposed to be, as nearly as possible, constructed upon the principle of the "wonderful one-horse shay." It was very essential that the animals be sturdy, whether oxen, mules or horses. Oxen were preferred as they were less liable to stampede or be stolen by Indians and for long hauls held out better and though slower they were steady and in the long run performed the journey in an equally brief time. Besides, in an emergency they could be used as beef. When possible the provisions and ammunition were protected from water and dust by heavy canvas or rubber sheets.

Good health, and above all, not too large a proportion of women and children was also taken into consideration. The morning starts had to be made early—always before six o'clock—and it would be hard to get children ready by that hour. Later on experience taught the mothers that in order not to delay the trains it was best to allow the smaller children to sleep in the wagons until after several hours of travel when they were taken up for the day.

Our caravan had a good many women and children and although we were probably longer on the journey owing to their presence—they exerted a good influence, as the men did not take such risks with Indians and thereby avoided conflict; were more alert about the care of the teams and seldom had accidents; more attention was paid to cleanliness and sanitation and, lastly but not of less importance, the meals were more regular and better cooked thus preventing much sickness and there was less waste of food.

Among those who formed the personnel of our train were the following families—a wonderful collection of many people with as many different dispositions and characteristics, all recognizing their mutual dependence upon each other and bound together by the single aim of "getting to California."

A regulation "prairie schooner" drawn by four oxen and well filled with suitable supplies, with two pack mules following on behind was the equipment of the Kenna family. There were two men, two women, a lad of fifteen years, a daughter thirteen and their half brother six weeks of age. This baby was our mascot and the youngest member of the company. . . .

Leaving Civilization

After a sufficient number of wagons and people were collected at this rendezvous we proceeded to draw up and agree upon a code of general regulations for train government and mutual protection—a necessary precaution when so many were to travel together. Each family was to be independent yet a part of the grand unit and every man was expected to do his individual share of general work and picket duty.

John Brophy was selected as Colonel. He was particularly eligible having served in the Black Hawk War and as much of his life had been spent along the frontier his experience with Indians was quite exceptional. . . .

It took us four days to organize our company of 70 wagons and 120 persons; bring our wagons and animals to the highest possible standard of preparedness; wash our clothes;

soak several days' supply of food—and say good-bye to civilization at Council Bluffs. Owing to the cheapness of eggs and chickens we reveled in their luxuries, carrying a big supply, ready cooked with us.

On May 26th we started to cross the Missouri River and our first real work affronted us.

Chapter 3

The Journey

HISTORY
HF
FIRSTHAND

Chapter Preface

Before 1841 most settlers traveled to California and the Pacific coast by sea. Books and newspaper reports from explorers and visitors to the far west roused the public's interest in an overland route. One trapper, Antoine Robidoux, who returned from California, described it as "a perfect paradise, a perpetual spring." One of the first organized overland wagon trains left the Missouri frontier in May 1841 with seventy people and a dozen wagons bound for the Pacific. By 1846 thousands of pioneers were taking the overland route west. By the 1850s the trails west were becoming so well traveled that in some places they were more than a mile wide.

Despite the glowing reports of the earthly Edens to be found in California and Oregon, the pioneers soon found the route to paradise was a hard six-month journey. Many rivers had to be crossed. The oxen, mules, and cattle had to swim through these waters while the wagons floated across. Water was always a problem. Too much rain caused the wagons to bog down in mud. However, droughts caused the cattle to die of thirst. Hundreds of travelers were infected with cholera at overcrowded wells. As the trail approached the mountains, ropes and pulleys were needed to pull the wagons up the steep paths. The overland journey could be made only in spring and summer. Any late starts or delays could be disastrous. If the wagon trains did not get across the mountains before the snow came, the settlers could become trapped and face starvation.

The trail had its daily difficulties, including buffalo stampedes, Indian scares, loss of cattle, wagon breakdowns, births, and deaths. Yet despite these hardships, most pioneers made it to their destinations and began new lives.

Trials Along the Trail

Amelia Stewart Knight

Amelia Stewart Knight, her husband, and seven children set out from Iowa bound for Oregon on April 9, 1853. There were rivers to cross, floods, storms, poisoned water, drought, and disease to endure. One child, Chatfield, caught scarlet fever and was almost run over by a wagon, and another child was left behind by mistake for a few hours at a campsite. In her diary, Amelia records all her daily trials with honesty and bravery.

On September 13 the Knights arrived on the west side of the Cascade Mountains, and four days later they had reached their destination. Soon after arrival, Amelia gave birth to her eighth child. The names of the children that made the journey were Plutarch, Seneca, Frances, Jefferson, Lucy, Almira, Chatfield, and finally Wilson. Amazingly, Amelia made no mention of her pregnancy in her diary until the day of Wilson's birth. Amelia never complains. She meets every danger to her family's survival with an irrepressible spirit. She is emblematic of the character of the pioneer woman without which the great migration west could never have been accomplished.

Starting from Monroe County, Iowa, Saturday, April 9, 1853, and ending Near Milwaukie, Oregon Territory, September 17, 1853.

Saturday, April 9, 1853 Started from home about 11 o'clock and traveled 8 miles and camped in an old house; night cold and frosty.

Sunday, April 10th Cool and pleasant, road hard and

Excerpted from "Diary of Mrs. Amelia Stewart Knight," by Amelia Stewart Knight, in *Women's Diaries of the Westward Journey*, edited by Lillian Schlissel (New York: Schocken Books, 1982).

dusty. Evening—Came 8½ miles and camped close to the Fulkersons' house.

Monday, April 11th Morn. Cloudy and sign of rain, about 10 o'clock it began to rain. At noon it rains so hard we turn out and camp in a school house after traveling 11½ miles; rains all the afternoon and all night, very unpleasant. Jefferson and Lucy have the mumps. Poor cattle bawled all night. . . .

Thursday, April 14th Quite cold. Little ewes crying with cold feet. Sixteen wagons all getting ready to cross the creek. Hurrah and bustle to get breakfast over. Feed the cattle. Hurrah boys, all ready, we will be the first to cross the creek this morning. Gee up Tip and Tyler, and away we go the sun just rising. Evening—We have traveled 24 miles today and are about to camp in a large prairie without wood. Cold and chilly; east wind. The men have pitched the tent and are hunting something to make a fire to get supper. I have the sick headache and must leave the boys to get it themselves the best they can. . . .

Saturday, April 16th Camped last night three miles east of Chariton Point in the prairie. Made our beds down in the tent in the wet and mud. Bed clothes nearly spoiled. Cold and cloudy this morning, and every body out of humour. Seneca is half sick. Plutarch has broke his saddle girth. Husband is scolding and hurrying all hands (and the cook) and Almira says she wished she was home, and I say ditto. "Home, Sweet Home.". . .

Crossing Rivers

Friday, May 6th . . . Here we passed a train of wagons on their way back, the head man had been drowned a few days before, in a river called Elkhorn, while getting some cattle across and his wife was lying in the wagon quite sick, and children were mourning for the father gone. With sadness and pity I passed those who perhaps a few days before had been well and happy as ourselves. Came 20 miles today.

Saturday, May 7th Cold morning, thermometer down to 48 in the wagon. No wood, only enough to boil some coffee. Good grass for the stock. We have crossed a small creek, with a narrow Indian bridge across it. Paid the Indians 75 cents toll. My hands are numb with cold. . . .

Sunday, May 8th Still in camp. Waiting to cross [the Elkhorn River]. There are three hundred or more wagons in sight and as far as the eye can reach, the bottom is covered, on each side of the river, with cattle and horses. There is no ferry here and the men will have to make one out of the tightest wagon-bed (every company should have a waterproof wagon-bed for this purpose.) Everything must now be hauled out of the wagons head over heels (and he who knows where to find anything will be a smart fellow.) then the wagons must be all taken to pieces, and then by means of a strong rope stretched across the river with a tight wagon-bed attached to the middle of it, the rope must be long enough to pull from one side to the other, with men on each side of the river to pull it. In this way we have to cross everything a little at a time. Women and children last, and then swim the cattle and horses. There were three horses and some cattle drowned while crossing this place yesterday. It is quite lively and merry here this morning and the weather fine. We are camped on a large bottom, with the broad, deep river on one side of us and a high bluff on the other. . . .

Storm

Friday, May 13th It is thundering and bids fair for rain. Crossed the river early this morning before breakfast. (Got breakfast over after a fashion. Sand all around ankle deep; wind blowing; no matter, hurry it over. Them that eat the most breakfast eat the most sand. . . .)

Saturday, May 14th . . . Winds so high that we dare not make a fire, impossible to pitch the tent, the wagons could hardly stand the wind. All that find room crowded into the wagons; those that can't, have to stay out in the storm. Some of the boys have lost their hats. . . .

Monday, May 16th Evening—We have had all kinds of weather today. This morning was dry, dusty and sandy. This afternoon it rained, hailed, and the wind was very high. Have been traveling all the afternoon in mud and water up to our hubs. Broke chains and stuck in the mud several times. The men and boys are all wet and muddy. Hard times but they say misery loves company. We are not alone on these bare plains, it is covered with cattle and wagons. . . .

Tuesday, May 17th We had a dreadful storm of rain and hail last night and very sharp lighting. It killed two oxen for one man. We have just encamped on a large flat prairie, when the storm commenced in all its fury and in two minutes after the cattle were taken from the wagons every brute was gone out of sight, cows, calves, horses, all gone before the storm like so many wild beasts. I never saw such a storm. The wind was so high I thought it would tear the wagons to pieces. Nothing but the stoutest covers could stand it. The rain beat into the wagons so that everything was wet, in less that 2 hours the water was a foot deep all over our camp grounds. As we could have no tents pitched, all had to crowd into the wagons and sleep in wet beds with their wet clothes on, without supper. The wind blew hard all night and this morning presents a dreary prospect surrounded by water, and our saddles have been soaking in it all night and are almost spoiled! . . .

Droves of Cattle

Tuesday, May 31st Evening—Traveled 25 miles today. When we started this morning there were two large droves of cattle and about 50 wagons ahead of us, and we either had to stay poking behind them in the dust or hurry up and drive past them. It was no fool of a job to be mixed up with several hundred head of cattle, and only one road to travel in, and the drovers threatening to drive their cattle over you if you attempted to pass them. They even took out their pistols. Husband came up just as one man held his pistol at Wilson Carl and saw what the fuss was and said, "Boys, follow me," and he drove our team out of the road entirely, and the cattle seemed to understand it all, for they went into the trot most of the way. The rest of the boys followed with their teams and the rest of the stock. I had rather a rough ride to be sure, but was glad to get away from such lawless set, which we did by noon. The head teamster done his best by whipping and hollowing to his cattle. He found it no use and got up into his wagon to take it easy. We left some swearing men behind us. We drove a good ways ahead and stopped to rest the cattle and eat some dinner. While we were eating we saw them coming. All hands jumped for their teams saying they had earned the road too dearly to let them pass us again, and in a few moments we were all on the go again. Had been very warm today. Thermometer at 98 in the wagon at one o'clock. Towards evening there came up a light thunderstorm which cooled the air down to 60. We are now within 100 miles of Fort Laramie [in Wyoming].

Wednesday, June 1st It has been raining all day long and we have been traveling in it so as to be able to keep ahead of the large droves. The men and boys are all soaking wet and look sad and comfortless. (The little ones and myself are shut up in the wagons from the rain. Still it will find its way in and many things are wet; and take us all together we are a poor looking set, and all this for Oregon. I am thinking while I write, "Oh, Oregon, you must be a wonderful country." Came 18 miles today.) . . .

Bad Water

Monday, June 6th Still in camp, husband and myself being sick (caused, we suppose by drinking the river water, as it looks more like dirty suds than anything else), we concluded to stay in camp and each take a vomit, which we did and are much better. The boys and myself have been washing some today. The prickly pear grows in great abundance along this Platte River road.

Tuesday, June 7th Rained some last night; quite warm today. Just passed Fort Laramie, situated on the opposite side of the river. This afternoon we passed a large village of Sioux Indians. Numbers of them came around our wagons. Some of the women had moccasins and beads, which they wanted to trade for bread. I gave the women and children all the cakes I had baked. Husband traded a big Indian a lot of hard crackers for a pair of moccasins and after we had started on he came up with us again making a great fuss, and wanted them back (they had eaten part of the crackers). He did not seem to be satisfied, or else he wished to cause us some trouble, or perhaps get into a fight. However, we handed the moccasins to him in a hurry and drove away from them as soon as possible. . . .

Tuesday, June 14th . . . Had a great deal of trouble to keep the stock from drinking the poison or alkali water. It is almost sure to kill man or beast who drink it.

Wednesday, June 15th . . . Passed Independence Rock [Wyoming] this afternoon, and crossed Sweetwater River on a bridge. Paid 3 dollars a wagon and swam the stock across. The river is very high and swift. . . .

Sick with Fever

Monday, July 4th It has been very warm today. Thermometer up to 110. . . . I never saw mosquitoes as bad as they are here. Chat has been sick all day with fever, partly caused by mosquitoe bites. . . .

Tuesday, July 5th . . . Chatfield is sick yet; had fever all night. . . .

Thursday, July 14th It is dust from morning until night, with now and then a sprinkling of gnats and mosquitoes, and as far as the eye can reach it is nothing but a sandy desert, covered with wild sage brush, dried up with heat; however, it makes good firewood. Evening—I have not felt well today and the road has been very tedious to me. I have ridden in the wagon and taken care of Chatfield till I got tired, then I got out and walked in the sand and through stinking sage brush till I gave out; and I feel thankful that we are about to camp after traveling 22 miles, on the bank of Raft River [in Idaho], about dark; river high. . . .

Monday, July 18th Traveled 22 miles. Crossed one small creek and have camped on one called Rock Creek. It is here the Indians are so troublesome. This creek is covered with small timber and thick underbrush, a great hiding place; and while in this part of the country the men have to guard the stock all night. One man traveling ahead of us had all his horses stolen and never found them as we know of. (I was very much frightened while at this camp. I lay awake all night. I expected every minute we would be killed. However, we all found our scalps on in the morning.) There are people killed at this place every year. . . .

Narrow Escape

Friday, July 22nd Crossed the river before daybreak and found the smell of carrion so bad that we left as soon as possible. The dead cattle were lying in every direction. Still there were a good many getting their breakfast among all the stench. I walked off among the rocks, while the men were getting the cattle ready; then we drove a mile or so, and halted to get breakfast. (Here Chat had a very narrow escape from being run over. Just as we were all getting ready to start, Chatfield the rascal, came around the forward wheel to get into the wagon and at that moment the cattle started and he fell under the wagon. Somehow he kept from under the wheels and escaped with only a good or I should say, a bad scare. I never was so much frightened in my life.) I was in the wagon at the time, putting things in order, and supposed Francis was taking care of him. . . .

Saturday, July 23rd We took a fresh start this morning with everything in order, for a good day's drive. Travel about 5 miles and here we are, up a stump again, with a worse place than we ever had before us to be crossed, called Bridge Creek. I presume it takes its name from a natural bridge which crosses it. This bridge is only wide enough to admit one person at a time. A frightful place, with the water roaring and tumbling ten or fifteen feet below it. This bridge is composed of rocks, and all around us, it is nothing but a solid mass of rocks, with the water ripping and tearing over them. Here we have to unload all the wagons and pack everything by hand, and then we are only on an island. There is a worse place to cross yet, a branch of the same. Have to stay on the island all night, and wait our turn to cross. . . .

Monday, July 25th Bad luck this morning to start with. A calf took sick and died before breakfast. Soon after starting one of our best cows was taken sick and died in a short time. Presumed they were both poisoned with water or weeds. Left our poor cow for the wolves and started on. . . .

Boiling Springs

Wednesday, July 27th Another fine cow died this afternoon. Came 15 miles today, and have camped at the boiling springs, a great curiosity. They bubble up out of the earth boiling hot. I have only to pour water on to my tea and it is made. There is no cold water in this part. (Husband and myself wandered far down this branch, as far as we dare, to find it cool enough to bathe in. It was still very hot, and I believe I never spent such an uneasy sleepless night in my life. I felt as if I was in the bad place. I still believe it was not very far off.) I was glad when morning came and we left.

Thursday, July 28th . . . Chat is quite sick with scarlet fever. . . .

Monday, August 1st This evening another of our best milk cows died. Cattle are dying off very fast all along this road. We are hardly ever out of sight of dead cattle, on this side of Snake River [in Idaho]. This cow was well and fat an hour before she died. Cut the second cheese today. . . .

Friday, August 5th . . . (Snake River Ferry) . . . Our turn to cross will come sometime tomorrow. There is one small ferry boat running here, owned by the Hudson's Bay Company. Have to pay three dollars a wagon. . . .

Lucy Left Behind

Monday, August 8th We have to make a drive of 22 miles, without water today. Have our cans filled to drink. Here we left unknowingly our Lucy behind, not a soul had missed her until we had gone some miles, when we stopped a while to rest the cattle; just then another train drove up behind us with Lucy. She was terribly frightened and so were some more of us when we found out what a narrow escape she had run. She said she was sitting under the bank of the river, when we started, busy watching some wagons cross, and did not know we were ready. And I supposed she was in Mr.

Carl's wagon, as he always took care of Francis and Lucy, and I took care of Myra and Chat, when starting he asked for Lucy, and Francis said "She is in Mother's wagon," as she often went there to have her hair combed. It was a lesson to all of us. Evening—It is near dark and we are still toiling on till we find a camping place. The little ones have curled down and gone to sleep without supper. Wind high, and it is cold enough for a great coat and mittens. . . .

Tuesday, September 6th Still in camp, washing and overhauling the wagons to make as light as possible to cross the mountains. Evening—After throwing away a good many things and burning up most of the deck boards of our wagons so as to lighten them, got my washing and cooking done and started on again. Crossed two branches, traveled 3 miles and have camped near the gate or foot of the Cascade Mountains (here I was sick all night, caused by my washing and working too hard). . . .

Thursday, September 8th Traveled 14 miles over the worst road that was ever made, up and down, very steep, rough and rocky hills, through mud holes, twisting and winding round stumps, logs and fallen trees. Now we are on the end of a log, now over a big root of a tree; now bounce down in a mud hole, then bang goes the other side of the wagon, and woe be to whatever is inside. There is very little chance to turn out of this road, on account of timber and fallen trees, for these mountains are a dense forest of pines, fir, white cedar or redwood (the handsomest timber in the world must be here in these Cascade Mountains). Many of the trees are 300 feet high and so dense to almost exclude the light of heaven, and for my own part I dare not look to the top of them for fear of breaking my neck. We have camped on a little stream called Sandy. No feed for the stock except flour and by driving them a mile or so, they can get a little swamp grass or pick brush.

Friday, September 9th Came eight and a half miles. Crossed Sandy 4 times; came over corduroy roads, through swamps, over rocks and hummocks, and the worst road that could be imagined or thought of, and have encamped about one o'clock in a little opening near the road. The men have driven the cattle a mile off from the road to try and find grass and rest them till morning. (We hear the road is still worse ahead.) There is a great deal of laurel growing here, which will poison the stock if they eat it. There is no end to the wagons, buggies, yokes, chains, etc. that are lying all along this road. Some splendid good wagons just left standing, perhaps with the owners names on them. and many the poor horses, mules, oxen, cows, etc. that are lying dead in these mountains. Afternoon—Slight shower. . . .

Journey's End

Tuesday, September 13th Ascended three steep, muddy hills this morning. Drove over some muddy, miry ground and through mud holes and have just halted at the first farm to noon and rest awhile and buy feed for the stock. Paid 1.50 per hundred for hay. Price of fresh beef 16 and 18 cts. per pound, butter ditto 1 dollar, eggs, 1 dollar a dozen, onion 4 and 5 dollars per bushel, all too dear for poor folks, so we have treated ourselves to some small turnips at the rate of 25 cents per dozen. Got rested and are now ready to travel again. . . . There we are in Oregon making our camp in an ugly bottom, with no home, except our wagons and tent. It is drizzling and the weather looks dark and gloomy. . . .

Wednesday, Sept. 14th Still in camp. Raining and quite disagreeable.

Thursday, Sept. 15th Still in camp and still raining. (I was sick all night.)

Friday, Sept. 17th In camp yet. Still raining. Noon—It has cleared off and we are all ready for a start again, for someplace we don't know where. . . .

A few days later my eighth child was born. After this we picked up and ferried across the Columbia River, utilizing skiff, canoes and flatboat to get across, taking three days to complete. Here husband traded two yoke of oxen for a half section of land with one-half acre planted to potatoes and a small log cabin and lean-to with no windows. This is the journey's end.

A Day on the Oregon Trail

Jesse Applegate

The restless urge to go west has been a way of life for Americans since Daniel Boone opened up the Cumberland Gap in 1775. The Oregon Trail became a popular route to a better life in the 1840s. Thousands ventured along the trail in caravans and parties. These pioneers sometimes formed large companies with captains, lieutenants, and pilots (navigators). One of the largest companies set out for Oregon in 1843 with almost a thousand pioneers and five thousand cattle. This group soon split into two. Jesse Applegate was the captain of the second group named the "Cow Column."

Applegate wrote this account for a reunion of Oregon pioneers. It is a fascinating glimpse into an eighteen-hour day on the trail. Applegate reveals that a wagon train was not a simple enterprise. They are many jobs to be done. Hunters go out in search of buffalo, scouts raise signal flags, herders tend to the cattle. On Applegate's journey there is a trial held at lunch to settle a legal dispute. In the evening, the wagons are circled and meals prepared. Music is heard and dancing begins. Overall, Applegate notes that only through cooperation of its members and strong, skillful leadership from its captain can the train make its way across the plains.

Applegate had been a successful farmer in Missouri when he made the decision to go west to Oregon. He knew some of the most important men who had pioneered the west— Captain William Clark, of the Lewis and Clark Expedition, and explorer Jedediah Smith. His decision to move west was

Excerpted from *Transactions of the Fourth Annual Reunion of the Oregon Pioneer Association for 1876*, by Jesse Applegate (Salem, OR: Oregon Pioneer Association, 1877).

no doubt influenced by these men. But an even stronger reason was his hatred of slavery which was condoned in Missouri. He thought slavery would have a bad effect on the moral principals of his six children. In Oregon, Jesse Applegate again took up farming. He also worked as a surveyor, schoolteacher, justice of the peace and served as a member of the territorial legislature.

It is four o'clock A.M.; the sentinels on duty have discharged their rifles—the signal that the hours of sleep are over; and every wagon and tent is pouring forth its night tenants, and slow-kindling smokes begin largely to rise and float away on the morning air. Sixty men start from the corral, spreading as they make through the vast herd of cattle and horses that form a semi-circle around the encampment, the most distant perhaps two miles away.

The herders pass to the extreme verge and carefully examine the trails beyond, to see that none of the animals have strayed or been stolen during the night. This morning no trails lead beyond the outside animals in sight, and by five o'clock the herders begin to contract the great moving circle and the well-trained animals move slowly toward camp, clipping here and there a thistle or tempting bunch of grass on the way. In about an hour five thousand animals are close up to the encampment, and the teamsters are busy selecting their teams and driving them inside the "corral" to be yoked. The corral is a circle one hundred yards deep, formed with wagons connected strongly with each other, the wagon in the rear being connected with the wagon in front by its tongue and ox chains. It is a strong barrier that the most vicious ox cannot break, and in case of an attack of the Sioux would be no contemptible entrenchment.

Breakfast

From six to seven o'clock is a busy time; breakfast is to be eaten, the tents struck, the wagons loaded, and the teams yoked and brought up in readiness to be attached to their respective wagons. All know when, at seven o'clock, the signal to march sounds, that those not ready to take their proper places in the line of march must fall into the dusty rear for the day.

There are sixty wagons. They have been divided into fifteen divisions or platoons of four wagons each, and each platoon is entitled to lead in its turn. The leading platoon of today will be the rear one tomorrow, and will bring up the rear unless some teamster, through indolence or negligence, has lost his place in the line, and is condemned to that uncomfortable post. It is within ten minutes of seven; the corral but now a strong barricade is everywhere broken, the teams being attached to the wagons. The women and children have taken their places in them. The pilot (a borderer who has passed his life on the verge of civilization, and has been chosen to the post of leader from his knowledge of the savage and his experience in travel through the roadless wastes) stands ready in the midst of the pioneers, and aids, to mount and lead the way. Ten or fifteen young men, not today on duty, form another cluster. They are ready to start a buffalo hunt, are well mounted, and well armed as they need be, for the unfriendly Sioux have driven the buffalo out of the Platte [River basin], and the hunters must ride fifteen or twenty miles to reach them. The cow drivers are hastening, as they get ready, to the rear of the charge, to collect and prepare them for the day's march.

It is on the stroke of seven; the rushing to and fro, the cracking of the whips, the loud command to oxen, and what seems to be the inextricable confusion of the last ten minutes has ceased. Fortunately every one has been found and every teamster is at his post. The clear notes of the trumpet sound in the front; the pilot and his guards mount their horses, the leading division of wagons move out of the encampment, and takes up the line of march, the rest fall into their places with the precision of clock work, until the spot so lately full of life sinks back into that solitude that seems to reign over the broad plain and rushing river as the caravan draws its lazy length toward the distant El Dorado. . . .

The caravan has been about two hours in motion and is

now extended as widely as a prudent regard for safety will permit. First, near the bank of the shining river, is a company of horsemen; they seem to have found an obstruction, for the main body has halted while three or four ride rapidly along the bank of the creek or slough. They are hunting a favorable crossing for the wagons; while we look they have succeeded; it has apparently required no work to make it passable, for all but one of the party has passed on and he has raised a flag, no doubt a signal to the wagons to steer their course to where he stands. The leading teamster sees

George Washington Bush on the Road to Oregon

In 1844 the British still had claim on the Columbia River Valley in present-day Washington. They opposed American settlement. But many American wagons trains ignored their claims. Colonel M.T. Simmons, an Irish immigrant, was one of the leaders of a wagon train headed for this sparsely settled territory. Another of the leaders of this expedition was George Washington Bush. He was an African American who had fought the British with Andrew Jackson in New Orleans. Neither Simmons nor Bush liked the idea that the British could tell them where to live.

Bush had become rich from cattle trading in Missouri and now wanted to settle in Oregon. But the Oregon legislature had passed a law that barred blacks from settling there. Simmons and Bush decided to settle north of the Columbia River on Puget Sound—outside the Oregon legislature's authority. John Minton was also traveling with this wagon train and wrote down this account.

I struck the road again in advance of my friends near Soda Springs. There was in sight, however, G.W. Bush, at whose camp table Rees and I had received the hospitalities of the Missouri rendezvous. Joining him, we went to the Springs. Bush was a mulatto, but had means, and also a white woman for a wife, and a family of five children. Not him though he is yet two miles off, and steers his course directly towards him, all the wagons following in his track. They (the wagons) form a line three quarters of a mile in length; some of the teamsters ride upon the front of their wagons, some walk beside their teams; scattered along the line companies of women and children are taking exercise on foot; they gather bouquets of rare and beautiful flowers that line the way; near them stalks a stately greyhound or an Irish wolf dog, apparently proud of keeping watch and ward over his master's wife and children.

---

many men of color left a slave state so well to do, and so generally respected; but it was not in the nature of things that he should be permitted to forget his color. As we went along together, he riding a mule and I on foot, he led the conversation to this subject. He told me he should watch, when we got to Oregon, what usuage was awarded to people of color, and if he could not have a free man's rights he would seek the protection of the Mexican Government in California or New Mexico. He said there were few in that train he would say as much to as he had just said to me. I told him I understood. This conversation enabled me afterwards to understand the chief reason for Col. M.T. Simmons and his kindred, and Bush and [Gabriel] Jones determining to settle north of the Columbia [River]. It was understood that Bush was assisting at least two of these to get to Oregon, and while they were all Americans, they would take no part in ill treating G.W. Bush on account of his color.

[Minton indicates that when the party heard rumors that any African American attempting to enter the Oregon Territory might be whipped, they agreed to fight to protect Bush.] No act of Colonel Simmons as a legislator was more creditable to him than getting Mr. Bush exempt from the Oregon law, intended to deter mulattoes or Negroes from settling in Oregon—a law, however, happily never enforced.

John Minton, "Reminiscences of Experiences on the Oregon Trail in 1844," *Quarterly of the Oregon Historical Society* 2, September 1901, pp. 212–13.

Next comes a band of horses; two or three men or boys follow them, the docile and sagacious animals scare needing their attention, for they have learned to follow in the rear of the wagons, and know that at noon they will be allowed to graze and rest. Their knowledge of the time seems as accurate as of the place they are to occupy in the line, and even a full-blown thistle will scarcely tempt them to straggle or halt until the dinner hour has arrived. Not so with the large herd of horned beasts that bring up the rear; lazy, selfish and unsocial, it has been a task to get them in motion, the strong always ready to domineer over the weak, halt in the front and forbid the weaker to pass them. They seem to move only in fear of the driver's whip; though in the morning full to repletion, they have not driven an hour before their hunger and thirst seem to indicate a fast of day's duration. Through all the long days their greed is never sated nor their thirst quenched, nor is there a moment of relaxation of the tedious and vexatious labors of their drivers, although to all others the march furnishes some season of relaxation or enjoyment. For the cow-drivers there is none. . . .

The Nooning Place

The pilot, by measuring the ground and timing the speed of the wagons and the walk of his horses, has determined the rate of each, so as to enable him to select the nooning place, as nearly as the requisite grass and water can be had at the end of five hours' travel of the wagons. Today, the ground being favorable, little time has been lost in preparing the road, so that he and his pioneers are at the nooning place an hour in advance of the wagons, which time is spent in preparing convenient watering places for the animals and digging little wells near the bank of the Platte. As the teams are not unyoked, but simply turned loose from the wagons, a corral is not formed at noon, but the wagons are drawn up in columns, four abreast, the leading wagon of each platoon on the left—the platoons being formed with that view. This brings friends together at noon as well as night.

Today an extra session of the Council is being held, to

settle a dispute that does not admit of delay, between a proprietor and a young man who has undertaken to do a man's
service on the journey for bed and board. Many such engagements exist and much interest is taken in the manner
this high court, from which there is no appeal, will define
the rights of each party in such engagements. The Council
was a high court in the most exalted sense. It was a Senate
composed of the ablest and most respected fathers of the
emigration. It exercised both legislative and judicial pow-
ers, and its laws and decisions proved it equal and worthy
of the high trust reposed in it. Its sessions were usually held
on days when the caravan was not moving. It first took the
state of the little commonwealth into consideration; revised
or repealed rules defective or obsolete, and exacted such
others as the exigencies seemed to require. The commonwealth being cared for, it next resolved itself into a court, to
hear and settle private disputes and grievances. The offender
and aggrieved appeared before it, witnesses were examined,
and the parties were heard by themselves and sometimes by
counsel. The judges thus being made fully acquainted with
the case, and being in no way influenced or cramped by
technicalities, decided all cases according to their merits.
There was but little use for lawyers before this court, for no
plea was entertained which was calculated to defeat the ends
of justice. Many of these judges have since won honors in
higher spheres. They have aided to establish on the broad
basis of right and universal liberty two of the pillars of our
great Republic in the Occident. Some of the young men who
appeared before them as advocates have themselves sat
upon the highest judicial tribunals, commanded armies, been
Governors of States, and taken high positions in the Senate
of the nation.

It is now one o'clock; the bugle has sounded, and the caravan has resumed its westward journey. It is in the same order, but the evening is far less animated than the morning
march; a drowsiness has fallen apparently on man and beast;
teamsters drop asleep on their perches and even walking by
their teams, and the words of command are now addressed

to the slowly creeping oxen in the softened tenor of women or the piping treble of children, while the snores of teamsters make a droning accompaniment. . . .

Evening Meal

The sun is now getting low in the west, and at length the painstaking pilot is standing ready to conduct the train in the circle which he has previously measured and marked out, which is to form the invariable fortification for the night. The leading wagons follow him so nearly round the circle, that but a wagon length separates them. Each wagon follows in its tracks, the rear closing on the front until its tongue and ox chains will perfectly reach from one to the other, and so accurate the measurement and perfect the practice, that the hindmost wagon of the train always precisely closes the gateway. As each wagon is brought into position it is dropped from its team (the teams being [pastured] inside the circle), the team unyoked, and the yokes and chains are used to connect the wagon strongly with that in its front. Within ten minutes from the time the leading wagon halted, the barricade is formed, the teams unyoked and driven out to pasture.

Everyone is busy preparing fires of buffalo chips to cook the evening meal, pitching tents and otherwise preparing for the night.

Braving the Desert

Sarah Royce

Sarah Royce, her husband, and her two-year-old daughter
made their way to California using only a handwritten diary
of a Mormon pioneer to navigate the trail. They left Salt Lake
City with three other men in their party. It was October and
they had to hurry to cross the Sierras before the snows closed
the passes. After making a wrong turn into the desert, they
nearly perished from lack of water and food. Luckily they
were found by a military relief party who helped them pack
their possessions onto mules in order to make the late crossing over the mountains. Unless the commander had disobeyed
orders and gone out of his way to assist them they would
surely have met a horrible fate.

In 1932, Royce wrote her memoir of her frontier experiences,
in which she recalled the peril of being lost in the desert.

We were traveling parallel with a placid river on our
right, beyond which were trees, and from us to the water's edge the ground sloped so gently it appeared absurd not
to turn aside to its brink and refresh ourselves and our oxen.

But as day dawned these beautiful sights disappeared, and
we began to look anxiously for the depression in the ground
and the holes dug which we were told would mark the Sink
of the Humboldt. But it was nearly noonday before we came
to them. There was still some passable water in the holes but
not fit to drink clear, so we contrived to gather enough sticks
of sage to boil some, made a little coffee, ate our lunch, and
thus refreshed, we hastened to find the forking road. Our di-

rector had told us that within about two or three miles beyond the Sink we might look for the road, to the left, and we
did look and kept looking and going on drearily till the sun
got lower and lower and night was fast approaching. Then
the conviction which had long been gaining ground in my
mind took possession of the whole party. We had passed the
forks of the road before daylight that morning and were now
miles out on the desert without a mouthful of food for the
cattle and only two or three quarts of water in a little cask.

What could be done? Halt we must, for the oxen were
nearly worn out and night was coming on. The animals must
at least rest, if they could not be fed, and that they might rest,
they were chained securely to the wagon, for hungry and
thirsty as they were, they would, if loose, start off frantically
in search of water and food and soon drop down exhausted.
Having fastened them in such a way that they could lie down,
we took a few mouthfuls of food and then, we in our wagon
and the men not far off upon the sand, fell wearily to sleep—
a forlorn little company wrecked upon the desert.

Out on the Desert

The first question in the morning was, "How can the oxen
be kept from starving?" A happy thought occurred. We had
thus far on our journey managed to keep something in the
shape of a bed to sleep on. It was a mattress tick, and just
before leaving Salt Lake we had put into it some fresh
hay—not very much, for our load must be as light as possible, but the old gentleman traveling with us had also a small
straw mattress; the two together might keep the poor things
from starving for a few hours. At once a small portion was
dealt out to them, and for the present they were saved. For
ourselves we had food which we believed would about last
us till we reached the gold mines if we could go right on; if
we were much delayed anywhere, it was doubtful. The two
or three quarts of water in our little cask would last only a
few hours, to give moderate drinks to each of the party. For
myself I inwardly determined I should scarcely take any of
it, as I had found throughout the journey that I could do with

less drink than most land travelers. Some of the men, however, easily suffered with thirst, and as to my little girl, it is
well known a child cannot do long without either water or
milk. Everything looked rather dark and dubious.

Should we try to go on? But there were miles of desert
before us, in which we knew neither grass or water could be
found. . . . Here we were without water and with only a few
mouthfuls of poor feed, while our animals were already
tired out and very hungry and thirsty. No, it would be mad-
ness to go farther out in the desert under such conditions.
Should we then turn back and try to reach the meadows with
their wells? But as near as we could calculate, it could not
be less than twelve or fifteen miles to them. Would it be possible for our poor cattle to reach there? Their only food
would be that pitiful mess still left in our mattresses. It
might be divided into two portions, giving them each a few
mouthfuls more at noon, and then if they kept on their feet
long enough to reach the holes at the Sink, we might possi-
bly find enough water to give them each a little drink, which
with the remainder of the fodder might keep them up till the
meadows were reached. It was a forlorn hope, but it was all
we had.

The morning was wearing away while these things were
talked over. Precious time was being wasted, but the truth
was the situation was so new and unexpected that it seemed
for a while to confuse—almost to stupefy—most of the little party, and those least affected in this way felt so deeply
the responsibility of the next move that they dared not de-
cide upon it hastily. . . . But this would never do. So the
more hopeful ones proposed that we should all eat something and as soon as the noon heat abated prepare for a
move. So we took some lunch, and soon the men were lying upon the sand at short distances from each other, fast
asleep. Soon some of the party awoke and after a little talk
concluded that two of them would walk to a bald ridge that
rose out of the flat waste about a mile and a half distant and
take a view from thence in the faint hope that we might yet
be mistaken and the forking road and the meadows might

still be in advance. My husband said he would go, and the best of the two young men went with him, while the other two wandered listlessly off again. I made no opposition; I felt no inclination to oppose, though I knew the helplessness and loneliness of the position would thus be greatly increased. But that calm strength, that certainty of One near and all-sufficient, hushed and cheered me. Only a woman who has been alone upon a desert with her helpless child can have any adequate idea of my experience for the next hour or two. But that consciousness of an unseen Presence still sustained me.

Turn Back!

When the explorers returned from their walk to the ridge, it was only to report no discovery, nothing to be seen on all sides but sand and scattered sagebrush interspersed with the carcasses of dead cattle. So there was nothing to be done but to turn back and try to find the meadows. Turn back! What a chill the words sent through one. *Turn back,* on a journey like that, in which every mile had been gained by most earnest labor, growing more and more intense until of late it had seemed that the certainty of *advance* with every step was all that made the next step possible. And now for miles we were to *go back.* In all that long journey no steps ever seemed so heavy, so hard to take, as those with which I turned my back to the sun that afternoon of October 4, 1849.

We had not been long on the move when we saw dust rising in the road at a distance and soon perceived we were about to meet a little caravan of wagons. Then a bright gleam of hope stole in. They had doubtless stopped at the meadows and were supplied with grass and water. Might it not be possible that they would have enough to spare for us? Then we could go on with them. My heart bounded at the thought. But the hope was short-lived. We met, and some of the men gathered round our wagon with eager inquiries, while those who could not leave their teams stood looking with wonder at a solitary wagon headed the wrong way.

Our story was soon told. It turned out that they were

camping in the meadows at the very time we passed the forking road without seeing it, the morning we so ambitiously started soon after midnight. Ah, we certainly got up too early that day! If we had only seen that road and taken it, we might now have been with this company, provided for the desert, and no longer alone. But when the question was asked whether they could spare sufficient grass and water to get our team over the desert, they shook their heads and unanimously agreed that it was out of the question. Their own cattle, they said, were weak from long travel and too often scant supplies. They had only been able to load up barely enough to get to the Carson River. The season was far advanced, and the clouds hanging of late round the mountaintops looked threatening. It would be like throwing away their own lives without any certainty of saving ours, for once out in the desert without food, we would all be helpless together. One of the men had his family with him, a wife and two or three children, and while they talked the woman was seen coming toward us. She had not, when they first halted, understood that any but men were with the lone wagon. As soon as she heard to the contrary and what were the circumstances, she hastened, with countenance full of concern, to condole with me, and I think, had the decision depended alone upon her, she would have insisted upon our turning back with them and sharing their feed and water to the last.

But fortunately for them, probably for us all, other counsels prevailed, and we resumed our depressing backward march. . . .

Grass and Water

I had now become so impressed with the danger of the cattle giving out that I refused to ride except for occasional brief rests. So, soon after losing sight of the dust of the envied little caravan, I left the wagon and walked the remainder of the day. For a good while I kept near the wagon, but by and by, being very weary, I fell behind. The sun had set before we reached the Sink, and the light was fading fast when the wagon disappeared from my sight behind a slight elevation, and as the others had gone on in advance some time before, I was all alone on the barren waste. However, as I recognized the features of the neighborhood and knew we were quite near the Sink, I felt no particular apprehension, only a feeling that it was a weird and dreary scene, and instinctively urged forward my tagging footsteps in hope of regaining sight of the wagon.

The next morning we resumed our backward march after feeding out the last mouthful of fodder. The water in the little cask was nearly used up in making coffee for supper and breakfast, but if only each one would be moderate in taking a share when thirst impelled him, we might yet reach the wells before anyone suffered seriously. We had lately had but few chances for cooking, and only a little boiled rice with dried fruit and a few bits of biscuit remained after we had done breakfast. If we could only reach the meadows by noon! But that we could hardly hope for; the animals were so weak and tired. There was no alternative, however; the only thing to be done was to go steadily on, determined to do and endure to the utmost.

I found no difficulty this morning in keeping up with the team. They went so slowly and I was so preternaturally stimulated by anxiety to get forward that before I was aware of it I would be some rods ahead of the cattle, straining my gaze as if expecting to see a land of promise, long before I had any rational hope of the kind. My imagination acted intensely. I seemed to see Hagar in the wilderness walking wearily away from her fainting child among the dried-up bushes and seating herself in the hot sand. I seemed to become Hagar myself, and when my little one from the wagon behind me called out "Mamma, I want a drink," I stopped, gave her some, noted that there were but a few swallows left, then mechanically pressed onward again, alone, repeating over and over the words "Let me not see the death of the child."

Wearily passed the hottest noonday hour, with many an anxious look at the horned heads which seemed to me to bow lower and lower, while the poor tired hoofs almost refused to move. The two young men had been out of sight for some time when all at once we heard a shout and saw, a few hundred yards in advance, a couple of hats thrown into the air and four hands waving triumphantly. As soon as we got near enough, we heard them call out "Grass and water! Grass and water!" and shortly we were at the meadows.

To Cross the Desert or Die

On Monday morning we loaded up, but did not hurry, for the cattle had not rested any too long; another day would have been better, but we dared not linger. So, giving them time that morning thoroughly to satisfy themselves with grass and water, we once more set forward toward the formidable desert and, at that late season, with our equipment, the scarcely less formidable Sierras. The feeling that we were once more going forward instead of backward gave an animation to every step which we could never have felt but by contrast. By night we were again at the Sink, where we once more camped, but we durst not, the following morning, launch out upon the desert with the whole day before us, for though it was now the 9th of October, the sun was still powerful for some hours daily, and the arid sand doubled its heat. Not much after noon, however, we ventured out upon the sea of sand, this time to cross or die. . . .

Morning was now approaching, and we hoped, when full daylight came, to see some signs of the river. But for two or three weary hours after sunrise nothing of the kind appeared. The last of the water had been given to the cattle before daylight. When the sun was up we gave them the remainder of their hay, took a little breakfast, and pressed forward. For a long time not a word was spoken save occasionally to the cattle. I had again unconsciously got in advance, my eyes scanning the horizon to catch the first glimpse of any change, though I had no definite idea in my mind what first to expect. But now there was surely something. Was it a cloud? It was very low at first, and I feared it might evaporate as the sun warmed it. But it became rather more distinct and a little higher. I paused and stood till the team came up. Then, walking beside it, I asked my husband what he thought that low dark line could be. "I think," he said, "it must be the timber on Carson River." Again we were silent, and for a while I watched anxiously the heads of the two leading cattle. They were rather unusually fine animals, often showing considerable intelligence, and so faithful had they been, through so many trying scenes, I could not help feeling a sort of attachment to them, and I pitied them as I observed how low their heads drooped as they pressed their shoulders so resolutely and yet so wearily against the bows. Another glance at the horizon. Surely there was now visible a little unevenness in the top of that dark line, as though it might indeed be trees. "How far off do you think that is now?" I said. "About five or six miles, I guess" was the reply. At that moment the white-faced leader raised his head, stretched forward his nose, and uttered a low moo-o-oo. I was startled, fearing it was the sign for him to fall, exhausted. "What is the matter with him?" I said. "I think he smells the water" was the answer. "How can he at such a distance?" As I spoke, the other leader raised his head stretched out his nose, and uttered the same sound. The hinder cattle seemed to catch the idea, whatever it was; they all somewhat increased their pace and from that time showed renewed animation.

At Carson River

But we had yet many weary steps to take, and noon had passed before we stood in the shade of those longed-for trees beside the Carson River. As soon as the yokes were removed, the oxen walked into the stream and stood a few moments, apparently enjoying its coolness, then drank as they chose, came out, and soon found feed that satisfied them for the present, though at this point it was not abundant. The remainder of that day was spent in much-needed rest. The next day we did not travel many miles, for our team showed decided signs of weakness, and the sand became deeper as we advanced, binding the wheels so as to make hauling very hard. We had conquered the desert.

But the great Sierra Nevada Mountains were still all before us, and we had many miles to make, up Carson River, before their ascent was fairly begun. If this sand continued many miles, as looked probable, when should we ever even begin the real climbing? The men began to talk among themselves about how much easier they could get on if they left the wagon, and it was not unlikely they would try starting out without us if we had to travel too slowly. But they could not do this to any real advantage unless they took with them their pack mule to carry some provisions. All they had was the bacon they found on the desert and some parched cornmeal, but they felt sanguine that they could go so much faster than the cattle with the wagon, they could easily make this last them through. But the bargain had been, when we agreed to supply them with flour, that the pack mule, and the old horse if he could be of any use, should be at our service to aid in any pinch that might occur, to the end of the journey. Having shared the perils of the way thus far, it certainly seemed unwise to divide the strength of so small a party when the mountains were to be scaled.

I wished most heartily there was some more rapid way for Mary and me to ride. But it was out of the question, for only a thoroughly trained mountain animal would do for me to ride, carrying her. Besides this, all the clothing and personal conveniences we had in the world were in our wagon, and we had neither a sufficient number of sound animals nor those of the right kind to pack them across the mountains. So the only way was to try to keep on. But it looked like rather a hopeless case when for this whole day we advanced but a few miles.

The next morning, Friday, the 12th of October, we set out once more, hoping the sand would become lighter and the road easier to travel. But instead of this the wheels sank deeper than yesterday, there was more of ascent to overcome, the sun shone out decidedly hot, and toward noon we saw that we were approaching some pretty steep hills, up which our road evidently led. It did not look as though we could ascend them, but we would at least try to reach their foot. As we neared them we saw dust rising from the road at one of the turns we could distinguish high up in the hills a few miles off. Probably it was some party ahead of us. There was no hope of our overtaking anybody, so when we lost sight of the dust we did not expect to see it again. But soon another section of the road was in sight, and again the dust appeared, this time nearer and plainly moving toward us. Conjecture now became very lively. It was probably Indians, but they could not be of the same tribes we had seen. Were they foes? How many were there? Repeatedly we saw the dust at different points but could make out no distinct figures.

Relief Company

We were now so near the foot of the hills that we could distinctly see a stretch of road leading down a very steep incline to where we were moving so laboriously along. Presently at the head of this steep incline appeared two horsemen clad in loose, flying garments that flapped like wings on each side of them, while their broad-brimmed hats, blown up from their foreheads, revealed hair and faces that belonged to no Indians. Their rapidity of motion and the steepness of the descent gave a strong impression of coming down from above, and the thought flashed into my mind, "They look heaven-sent." As they came nearer we saw that each of them led by a halter a fine mule, and the perfect ease with which all the animals cantered down that steep was a marvel in our eyes. My husband and myself were at the heads of the lead cattle, and our little Mary was up in the front of the wagon, looking with wonder at the approaching forms.

As they came near they smiled, and the forward one said, "Well, sir, you are the man we are after!" "How can that be?" said my husband with surprise. "Yes, sir," continued the stranger, "you and your wife and that little girl are what brought us as far as this. You see, we belong to the relief company sent out by order of the United States Government to help the late emigrants over the mountains. We were ordered only as far as Truckee Pass. When we got there we

met a little company that had just got in. They'd been in a
snowstorm at the summit—'most got froze to death themselves, lost some of their cattle, and just managed to get to
where some of our men had fixed a relief camp. There was
a woman and some children with them, and that woman set
right to work at us fellows to go on over the mountains after a family she said they'd met on the desert going back for
grass and water 'cause they'd missed their way. She said
there was only one wagon, and there was a woman and child
in it, and she knew they could never get through them
canyons and over them ridges without help. We told her we
had no orders to go any farther then. She said she didn't care
for orders. She didn't believe anybody would blame us for
doing what we were sent out to do, if we did have to go farther than ordered. And she kept at me so, I couldn't get rid
of her. You see, I've got a wife and little girl of my own, so
I felt just how it was, and I got this man to come with me,
and here we are, to give you more to eat, if you want it, let
you have these two mules, and tell you how to get right over
the mountains the best and quickest way."

While he thus rapidly, in cheery though blunt fashion, explained their sudden presence with us, the thought of their being heaven-sent—that had so lightly flashed into my mind as
I at first watched their rapid descent of the hill with flying garments—grew into a sweetly solemn conviction, and I stood
in mute adoration, breathing in my inmost heart thanksgiving
to that Providential hand which had taken hold of the con-
flicting movements, the provoking blunders, the contradic-
tory plans, of our lives and those of a dozen other people who
a few days before were utterly unknown to each other and
many miles apart, and had from those rough, broken materials wrought out for us so unlooked-for a deliverance.

Starvation and Death at Donner Lake

Virginia Reed Murphy

The final leg of the Oregon Trail, crossing the mountains into California and Oregon, tested the limits of the pioneers' endurance. The path into California, for example, was unmapped for many years. Different expeditions tried to find the best route through the Sierras at their own peril.

By 1846, the established, though arduous, route was the California Trail. In that year, three hundred pioneers took the California Trail over the Sierras, and most reached the Sacramento Valley without loss of life. But for the Donner-Reed Party everything went well until they reached Fort Bridger. There they decided to take a short cut to California described in Lansford W. Hastings' *Emigrants' Guide.* They soon discovered their choice was unfortunate. The terrain was steep and rocky, and the party was forced to abandon their over-loaded wagons. They lost weeks on the untested short cut, and this caused them to reach the Sierras late in the season. They added to their problems by fighting among themselves. On October 5, James Reed got into a fight with one of the teamsters and killed him with his knife. Reed was expelled from the train and set out on his own to California.

As the first snows began to fall, the party became snow-bound and trapped in the mountains. At one point, Charles Stanton, a thirty-five-year-old bachelor and merchant from Chicago, made it to the summit of the pass. But when he saw the rest could not follow, he turned back. They camped for the winter near a lake that would later be named Donner Lake.

From "Across the Plains in the Donner Party," by Virginia Reed Murphy, *Century Magazine*, 1891.

There they suffered from cold and lack of food. To survive, some had to resort to eating the flesh of those who had died. Meanwhile the ostracized James Reed reached California and organized and led the rescue party that returned for the trapped pioneers. Reed's actions saved his family and others in the wagon train. Unfortunately, of the eighty-nine persons who entered the mountains only half came out alive. The others died from cold and starvation.

Twelve-year-old Virginia Reed was a member of that fateful party to be trapped in the Sierras by early winter snows while crossing into California. She tells of the hardships, awful suffering and eventual rescue by her father. Reed, at the age of fifty-six, remembers these momentous events at the that have become an American epic.

Snow was already falling, although it was only the last week in October [1846]. Winter had set in a month earlier than usual. All trails and roads were covered, and our only guide was the summit, which it seemed we would never reach. Despair drove many nearly frantic. Each family tried to cross the mountains but found it impossible. When it was seen that the wagons could not be dragged through the snow, their goods and provisions were packed on oxen and another start was made, men and women walking in snow up to their waists, carrying their children in their arms and trying to drive their cattle. The Indians said they could find no road, so a halt was called, and Stanton went ahead with the guides and came back and reported that we could get across if we kept right on, but that it would be impossible if snow fell. He was in favor of a forced march until the other side of the summit should be reached, but some of our party were so tired and exhausted with the day's labor that they declared they could not take another step, so the few who knew the danger that the night might bring yielded to the many, and we camped within three miles of the summit.

That night came the dreaded snow. Around the campfires under the trees great feathery flakes came whirling down.

The air was so full of them that one could see objects only a few feet away. The Indians knew we were doomed, and one of them wrapped his blanket about him and stood all night under a tree. We children slept soundly on our cold bed of snow with a soft white mantle falling over us so thickly that every few moments my mother would have to shake the shawl—our only covering—to keep us from being buried alive. In the morning the snow lay deep on mountain and valley. With heavy hearts we turned back to a cabin that had been built by the Murphy-Schallenberger party two years before. We built more cabins and prepared as best we could for the winter. That camp, which proved the camp of death to many in our company, was made on the shore of a lake, since known as Donner Lake. The Donners were camped in Alder Creek Valley below the lake and were, if possible, in a worse condition than ourselves. The snow came on so suddenly that they had no time to build cabins, but hastily put up brush sheds, covering them with pine boughs.

Three double cabins were built at Donner Lake, which were known as the Breen Cabin, the Murphy Cabin, and the Reed-Graves Cabin. The cattle were all killed, and the meat was placed in snow for preservation. My mother had no cattle to kill, but she made arrangements for some, promising to give two for one in California. Stanton and the Indians made their home in my mother's cabin.

Forlorn Hope

Many attempts were made to cross the mountains, but all who tried were driven back by the pitiless storms. Finally a party was organized, since known as the Forlorn Hope. They made snowshoes, and fifteen started—ten men and five women—but only seven lived to reach California; eight men perished. They were over a month on the way, and the horrors endured by that Forlorn Hope no pen can describe nor imagination conceive. The noble Stanton was one of the party and perished the sixth day out, thus sacrificing his life for strangers. I can find no words in which to express a fitting tribute to the memory of Stanton.

The misery endured during those four months at Donner Lake in our little dark cabins under the snow would fill pages and make the coldest heart ache. Christmas was near, but to the starving its memory gave no comfort. It came and passed without observance, but my mother had determined weeks before that her children should have a treat on this one day. She had laid away a few dried apples, some beans, a bit of tripe, and a small piece of bacon. When this hoarded store was brought out, the delight of the little ones knew no bounds. The cooking was watched carefully, and when we sat down to our Christmas dinner, Mother said, "Children, eat slowly, for this one day you can have all you wish." So bitter was the misery relieved by that one bright day that I have never since sat down to a Christmas dinner without my thoughts going back to Donner Lake.

The storms would often last ten days at a time, and we would have to cut chips from the logs inside which formed our cabins in order to start a fire. We could scarcely walk, and the men had hardly strength to procure wood. We would drag ourselves through the snow from one cabin to another, and some mornings snow would have to be shoveled out of the fireplace before a fire could be made. Poor little children were crying with hunger, and mothers were crying because they had so little to give their children. We seldom thought of bread, we had been without it so long. Four months of such suffering would fill the bravest hearts with despair. . . .

Another Desperate Attempt

Time dragged slowly along till we were no longer on short allowance but were simply starving. My mother determined to make an effort to cross the mountains. She could not see her children die without trying to get them food. It was hard to leave them, but she felt that it must be done. She told them she would bring them bread, so they were willing to stay, and with no guide but a compass we started—my mother, Eliza, Milt Elliott, and myself. Milt wore snow-shoes, and we followed in his tracks. We were five days in the mountains; Eliza gave out the first day and had to return, but we kept on and climbed one high mountain after another only to see others higher still ahead. Often I would have to crawl up the mountains, being too tired to walk. The nights were made hideous by the screams of wild beasts heard in the distance. Again, we would be lulled to sleep by the moan of the pine trees, which seemed to sympathize with our loneliness. One morning we awoke to find ourselves in a well of snow. During the night, while in the deep sleep of exhaustion, the heat of the fire had melted the snow and our little camp had gradually sunk many feet below the surface until we were literally buried in a well of snow. The danger was that any attempt to get out might bring an avalanche upon us, but finally steps were carefully made and we reached the surface. My foot was badly frozen, so we were compelled to return, and just in time, for that night a storm came on, the most fearful of the winter, and we should have perished had we not been in the cabins.

Nothing to Eat but Raw Hides

We now had nothing to eat but raw hides, and they were on the roof of the cabin to keep out the snow; when prepared for cooking and boiled they were simply a pot of glue. When the hides were taken off our cabin and we were left without shelter, Mr. Breen gave us a home with his family, and Mrs. Breen prolonged my life by slipping me little bits of meat now and then when she discovered that I could not eat the hide. Death had already claimed many in our party, and it seemed as though relief never would reach us. Baylis Williams, who had been in delicate health before we left Springfield, was the first to die; he passed away before starvation had really set in. . . .

Failed Rescue

On his arrival at Sutter's Fort my father made known the situation of the emigrants, and Captain Sutter offered at once to do everything possible for their relief. He furnished horses and provisions, and my father and Mr. McClutchen started for the mountains, coming as far as possible with horses and then with packs on their backs proceeding on foot; but they were finally compelled to return. Captain Sutter was not surprised at their defeat. He stated that there were no able-bodied men in that vicinity, all having gone down the country with Frémont to fight the Mexicans. He advised my father to go to Yerba Buena, now San Francisco, and make his case known to the naval officer in command. My father was in fact conducting parties there—when the seven members of the Forlorn Hope arrived from across the mountains. Their famished faces told the story. Cattle were killed and men were up all night, drying beef and making flour by hand mills, nearly two hundred pounds being made in one night, and a party of seven, commanded by Captain Reasen P. Tucker, were sent to our relief by Captain Sutter and the alcalde, Mr. Sinclair.

"Relief, Thank God, Relief!"

On the evening of February 19, 1847, they reached our cabins, where all were starving. They shouted to attract attention. Mr. Breen clambered up the icy steps from our cabin, and soon we heard the blessed words, "Relief, thank God, relief!" There was joy at Donner Lake that night, for we did not know the fate of the Forlorn Hope, and we were told that relief parties would come and go until all were across the mountains. But with the joy sorrow was strangely blended. There were tears in other eyes than those of children; strong men sat down and wept. For the dead were lying about on the snow, some even unburied, since the living had not had strength to bury their dead. When Milt Elliott died—our faithful friend who seemed so like a brother—my mother and I dragged him up out of the cabin and covered him with snow. Commencing at his feet, I patted the pure white snow down softly until I reached his face. Poor Milt! It was hard to cover that face from sight forever, for with his death our best friend was gone.

On the 22nd of February the first relief started with a party of twenty-three—men, women, and children. My mother and her family were among the number. It was a bright, sunny morning, and we felt happy, but we had not gone far when Patty and Tommy gave out. They were not able to stand the fatigue, and it was not thought safe to allow them to proceed, so Mr. Glover informed Mama that they would have to be sent back to the cabins to await the next expedition. What language can express our feelings? My mother said that she would go back with her children—that we would all go back together. This the relief party would not permit, and Mr. Glover promised Mama that as soon as they reached Bear Valley he himself would return for her children. . . . Mr. Glover returned with the children and, providing them with food, left them in the care of Mr. Breen.

With sorrowful hearts we traveled on, walking through the snow in single file. The men wearing snowshoes broke the way, and we followed in their tracks. At night we lay down on the snow to sleep, to awake to find our clothing all frozen, even to our shoestrings. At break of day we were again on the road, owing to the fact that we could make better time over the frozen snow. The sunshine, which it would seem would have been welcome, only added to our misery. The dazzling reflection of the snow was very trying to the eyes, while its heat melted our frozen clothing, making [it] cling to our bodies. My brother was too small to step in the tracks made by the men, and in order to travel he had to place his knee on the little hill of snow after each step and climb over. Mother coaxed him along, telling him that every step he took he was getting nearer Papa and nearer something to eat. He was the youngest child that walked over the Sierra Nevada. On our second day's journey John Denton gave out and declared it would be impossible for him to travel, but he begged his companions to continue their journey. A fire was built and he was left lying on a bed of freshly cut pine boughs, peacefully smoking. He looked so comfortable that my little brother wanted to stay with him, but when the second relief party reached him, poor Denton was past waking. His last thoughts seemed to have gone back to his childhood's home, as a little poem was found by his side, the pencil apparently just dropped from his hand.

Second Relief and Reunion

Captain Tucker's party on their way to the cabins had lightened their packs of a sufficient quantity of provisions to supply the sufferers on their way out. But when we reached the place where the cache had been made by hanging the food on a tree, we were horrified to find that wild animals had destroyed it, and again starvation stared us in the face. But my father was hurrying over the mountains and met us in our hour of need with his hands full of bread. He had expected to meet us on this day and had stayed up all night, baking bread to give us. He brought with him fourteen men. Some of his party were ahead, and when they saw us coming they called out: "Is Mrs. Reed with you? If she is, tell her Mr. Reed is here." We heard the call; Mother knelt on the snow, while I tried to run to meet Papa.

When my father learned that two of his children were still at the cabins, he hurried on, so fearful was he that they might perish before he reached them. He seemed to fly over the snow and made in two days the distance we had been five in traveling and was overjoyed to find Patty and Tommy alive. He reached Donner Lake on the 1st of March, and what a sight met his gaze! The famished little children and the deathlike look of all made his heart ache. He filled Patty's apron with biscuits, which she carried around, giving one to each person. He had soup made for the infirm and rendered every assistance possible to the sufferers. Leaving them with about seven days' provisions, he started out with a party of seventeen, all that were able to travel. Three of his men were left at the cabins to procure wood and assist the helpless. My father's party (the second relief) had not traveled many miles when a storm broke upon them. With the snow came a perfect hurricane. The crying of half-frozen children, the lamenting of the mothers, and the suffering of the whole party was heartrending; and above all could be heard the shrieking of the storm king. One who has never witnessed a blizzard in the Sierra can form no idea of the situation. All night my father and his men worked unceasingly through the raging storm, trying to erect shelter for the dying women and children. At times the hurricane would burst forth with such violence that he felt alarmed on account of the tall timber surrounding the camp. The party were destitute of food, all supplies that could be spared having been left with those at the cabins. The relief party had cached provisions on their way over to the cabins, and my father had sent three of the men forward for food before the storm set in, but they could not return. Thus, again, death stared all in the face. At one time the fire was nearly gone; had it been lost, all would have perished. Three days and nights they were exposed to the fury of the elements. Finally my father became snow-blind and could do no more, and he would have died but for the exertions of William McClutchen and Hiram Miller, who worked over him all night. From this time forward the toil and responsibility rested upon McClutchen and Miller.

The storm at last ceased, and these two determined to set out over the snow and send back relief to those not able to travel. Hiram Miller picked up Tommy and started. Patty thought she could walk, but gradually everything faded from her sight, and she too seemed to be dying. All other sufferings were now forgotten, and everything was done to revive the child. My father found some crumbs in the thumb of his woolen mitten; warming and moistening them between his own lips, he gave them to her and thus saved her life, and afterward she was carried along by different ones in the company. Patty was not alone in her travels. Hidden away in her bosom was a tiny doll, which she had carried day and night through all of our trials. Sitting before a nice, bright fire at Woodworth's Camp, she took dolly out to have a talk and told her of all her new happiness.

The Indomitable Spirit of the Second Handcart Company

Daniel D. McArthur

In the 1850s intensive missionary work in England and Europe produced a flood of converts to Mormonism. These new converts were eager to cross ocean, rivers, and plains to get to the New Zion in Salt Lake City. Thousands arrived on the East Coast and traveled by rail to the jumping-off point at Council Bluffs, Iowa on the Missouri River. Most of these pioneers were very poor. The Mormon Church set up an immigration fund to assist the new "saints" as the Mormons called their members. When wagons became too expensive, Brigham Young, the Mormon leader, decided to provide the settlers with handcarts to transport their possessions. These "handcart pioneers" as they were called walked and pulled their handcarts on the thousand-mile journey to Salt Lake City. The handcart companies also included a few covered wagons pulled by oxen.

This account is from the "Report on the Second Handcart Company." It was written in 1856 by one of the leaders of the company, Daniel D. McArthur. The Second Handcart Company had 222 members. The report recounts the events of one day when two members of the company were injured. Both were women, over sixty, and close friends. Mary Bathgate was bitten by a large rattlesnake. Mary was recuperating in one of the wagons when her friend Isabella Park tried to visit her and

From "Captain McArthur's Report on the Second Handcart Company," by Daniel D. McArthur, in *Handcarts to Zion*, edited by Leroy R. Hafen (Glendale, CA: Arthur H. Clark Company, 1960).

was accidentally run over by the wheels of the two-ton wagon. Isabella was not seriously hurt. As they recuperated, they rode together, suffered together, and comforted one another. Soon they were back on the trail walking side by side toward Salt Lake City. Their story embodies the indomitable spirit and mutual support that bought the "handcart pioneers" across the plains and into Utah.

On the 19th of May, 1856, our company, which had crossed the sea with us, were divided, by President Daniel Spencer, into two handcart companies, Brother Edmond Ellsworth to take charge of the first and I, Daniel D. McArthur, to take charge of the second company. Then every move was made to get our carts ready, which job was a tedious one, but by using all our efforts, the first company was enabled to start on the 9th of June, and the second on the 11th, about 11 o'clock. This second company numbered 222 souls, and were bound for Florence [in Nebraska], and from thence to the Valley, at which place (Florence) we arrived on the 8th day of July, distance, 300 miles, or there abouts. We had the very best of good luck all the way, although the weather was very hot and sweltering, but let me tell you, the saints were not to be overcome. Our carts, when we started, were in an awful fix. They moaned and growled, screeched and squealed, so that a person could hear them for miles. You may think this is stretching things a little too much, but it is a fact, and we had them to eternally patch, mornings, noons and nights. But by our industry we got them all along to Florence, and being obliged to stop at Florence some two weeks to get our outfit for the plains, I and my council, namely, Truman Leonard and Spencer Crandall, went to work and gave our carts a thorough repair throughout, and on the 24th of July, at 12 o'clock, we struck our tents and started for the plains, all in the best of spirits. Nothing but the very best of luck attended us continually. Our train consisted of 12 yoke of oxen, 4 wagons, and 48 carts; we also had 5 beef and 12 cows; flour, 55 lbs. per head, 100 lbs. rice, 550 lbs. sugar, 400 lbs. dried apples, 125 lbs. tea, and 200 lbs. salt for the company. On the 28th of August, we arrived at Laramie [Wyoming], and on the 2nd of September we met the first provision wagons from the Valley. On Deer Creek we got 1000 lbs. of flour, which caused the hearts of the saints to be cheered up greatly. On the 14th we camped at Pacific Spring Creek, and there I took in 1000 lbs. of more flour, so as to be sure to have enough to do me until we got into the Valley, for I was told that that would be the last opportunity to get it. On the 20th we reached Fort Bridger, and on the 26th of September, we arrived in this Valley, with only the loss of 8 souls. 7 died, and one, a young man, age 20 years, we never could tell what did become of him. We brought in our 48 carts, 4 wagons, 12 yokes of oxen, save one, which we had left at Fort Bridger, 10 cows, (one cow died and one we left at Fort Bridger,) and the 5 beeves, we ate, of course. We laid still 5 Sundays and three week days all day, besides other short stops while traveling from the Missouri River here.

My company was divided into two divisions and Brother Truman Leonard was appointed captain over the first division and Brother Spencer Crandall over the second. We had six tents in each division and a president over each tent, who were strict in seeing that singing and prayer was attended to every morning and night, and that peace prevailed. I must say that a better set of saints to labor with I never saw. They all did the best they could to forward our journey. When we came to a stream, no matter how large it might be, the men would roll up their trousers and into it they would go, and the sisters would follow, if the men were smart enough to get ahead of them, which the men failed many times to do. If the water was high enough to wet the things on the carts, the men would get one before the cart and one behind it and lift it up slick and clean, and carry it across the stream.

Snakebite

I will state a couple of incidents that happened in one day, and one other circumstance that took place. On the 11th of August a man came to camp pretending to be starved nearly to death, and wished me to give him some provisions, for he had had nothing for many days but what he had hunted for. So I gave him bread and meat enough to last him some four or five days and he acted as though he had met with some friends indeed. He said, that he had been robbed by some Californians somewhere near Fort Bridger, with whom he was in company on their way to the States, and on the 16th, while crossing over some sand hills, Sister Mary Bathgate was badly bitten by a large rattlesnake, just above the ankle, on the back part of her leg. She was about a half a mile ahead of the camp at the time it happened, as she was the ring leader of the footmen or those who did not pull the handcarts. She was generally accompanied by Sister Isabella Park. They were both old women, over 60 years of age, and neither of them had ridden one inch, since they had left Iowa camp ground. Sister Bathgate sent a little girl back to me as quickly as possible to have me and Brothers Leonard and Crandall come with all haste, and bring the oil with us, for she was bitten badly. As soon as we heard the news, we left all things, and, with the oil, we went post haste. When we got to her she was quite sick, but said that there was power in the Priesthood, and she knew it. So we took a pocket knife and cut the wound larger, squeezed out all the bad blood we could, and there was considerable, for she had forethought enough to tie her garter around her leg above the wound to stop the circulation of the blood. We then took and anointed her leg and head, and laid our hands on her in the name of Jesus and felt to rebuke the influence of the poison, and she felt full of faith. We then told her that she must get into the wagon, so she called witnesses to prove that she did not get into the wagon until she was compelled to by the cursed snake. We started on and traveled about two miles, when we stopped to take some refreshments. Sister Bathgate continued to be quite sick, but was full of faith, and after stopping one and a half hours we hitched up our teams.

As the word was given for the teams to start, old Sister Isabella Park ran in before the wagon to see how her companion was. The driver, not seeing her, hallooed at his team and they being quick to mind, Sister Park could not get out of the way, and the fore wheel struck her and threw her down and passed over both her hips. Brother Leonard grabbed hold of her to pull her out of the way, before the hind wheel could catch her. He only got her out part way and the hind wheels passed over her ankles. We all thought that she would be all mashed to pieces, but to the joy of us all, there was not a bone broken, although the wagon had something like two tons burden on it, a load for 4 yoke of oxen. We went right to work and applied the same medicine to her that we did to the sister who was bitten by the rattlesnake, and although quite sore for a few days, Sister Park got better, so that she was on the tramp before we got into this Valley, and Sister Bathgate was right by her side, to cheer her up. Both were as smart as could be long before they got here, and this is what I call good luck, for I know that nothing but the power of God saved the two sisters and they traveled together, they rode together, and suffered together. Sister Bathgate has got married since she arrived in the Valley. While we were leading our handcart companies through the States and on the plains, we were called tyrants and slave drivers, and everything else that could be thought of, both by Gentiles and apostates.

Chapter 4

Encountering Native Americans

Chapter Preface

O ne of the greatest fears of the pioneers was attack by Indians. Much of the worry, however, was unfounded. The vast majority of the pioneers never encountered hostile tribes. In fact, during the early years of migration the Native Americans were very helpful to the pioneers traveling west. Indians helped guide many wagon trains through the mountain passes. They were also experts at getting cattle and wagons across rivers. They even supplied the wagon trains with fresh horses, though the price could be quite high. Meriwether Lewis and William Clark would never have made it across the Rocky Mountains without assistance from the Shoshone. Sacagawea, a Shoshone woman, guided Lewis and Clark up the Missouri River as far as their boats would carry them. She also secured horses from her brother, a Shoshone chief, so that Lewis and Clark were able to continue across the mountains.

Encounters with Native Americans along the trail were frequent and most often peaceful. The pioneers traded their tobacco, clothes, tools, and guns for the Indians' buffalo meat and dried salmon. However, as the pioneers grew more numerous, the Native Americans felt their way of life was threatened. The pioneers slaughtered the buffalo, and their cattle ate the grass and exhausted water holes. The Indians began to demand tolls for crossing bridges and for safe passage through their lands. Violence was usually the result when pioneers resisted paying these fees. Indians often took revenge on later wagon trains. The pioneers began demanding military protection, and the cycle of violence grew.

At night the wagon trains circled around a campsite, forming a protective enclosure. Indian war parties rarely attacked a circle of wagons. When they did attack, it was on small parties or on individuals. Some massacres occurred, but on the whole, little pioneer blood was shed. Between 1840 and 1860 one historian estimated that Native Americans killed 362 pioneers. This is a small number compared to a much larger death toll of over ten thousand from everyday dangers such as disease and accidents along the trail. Generally, the pioneers had little to fear from encounters with Native Americans, except a few stolen cattle.

Avoiding Confrontation

Lansford W. Hastings

In 1842, Lansford W. Hastings joined a party of sixty emigrants bound for Oregon. At Independence Rock in Wyoming, Hastings and a fellow emigrant, Mr. Lovejoy, were writing their names on the landmark when they were confronted by a small group of Indians. They tried to flee but were captured by a larger force of Indians and taken to their village. Hastings managed to persuade the Indians to take them back to the wagon train where they exchanged gifts, traded and smoked the "pipe of peace" avoiding any bloodshed.

This incident is taken from Hastings' *Emigrants' Guide to Oregon and California* published in 1845. The guide was actually a commercial advertisement intended to promote emigration to California where Hastings had business and political interests. In his guide, Hastings portrayed California and Oregon as virtual paradises. He idealized both his own adventures and the character of the pioneers traveling west. He also cast the Native American and Mexican inhabitants of the area as lazy, dumb, and dishonest. While most pioneers were very afraid of Indian attacks, in reality, their fears were rarely realized. The vast majority of the encounters with Indian tribes were either friendly or ended much like the scene described by Hastings—with an exchange of gifts, goods, and food.

Excerpted from *The Emigrants' Guide to Oregon and California*, by Lansford W. Hastings (Bedford, MA: Applewood Books, 1994).

The company having left our unfortunate encampment, on Sweet-water, early in the morning, soon passed Independence Rock, which will be described, in the description of the routes. A Mr. Lovejoy and myself stopped at this rock, with a view of spending a few hours, in examining its peculiar structure, as well as to observe the various names, there to be seen, of individuals who have passed that way; and at the same time, to inscribe our own names, with the number of our company, the date of our passing; and whatever else might occur to us, as being serviceable to those who might subsequently pass that way. Having provided ourselves with materials for lettering, we tied our horses at the foot of this extraordinary rock, where we also left our guns, and commenced our toilsome assent up the rocky declivity. The company had, in the meantime, gone on, supposing that we would find no difficulty in overtaking them, whenever we had accomplished our purpose.

We had scarcely completed our labors, when we were surprised by the sudden appearance of seven Indians, who had descried us from some remote hill or mountain. They presented themselves to us, in the most hostile attitude, rushing towards us with the greatest vehemence; uttering the most terrific and demoniac yells; and with the most frightful gestures, seeming to design nothing but our immediate destruction. With drawn bows and guns, they thus rapidly advanced, while we were cautiously, yet hastily descending the rocky heights; winding our way with all possible haste, to the point at which we had left our guns and horses, at which place, ourselves and the Indians arrived at the same time, when we immediately seized our guns, with a view of defending ourselves. But upon seeing us take our guns, they at once lowered their bows and guns, and extended their hands in friendship. We hastily took their hands, but as hastily proceeded to mount, and to prepare for our departure. We had scarcely mounted, when they evinced a determination to prevent our leaving. One of them held Mr. Lovejoy's mule by the bit, while others laid hold of his person; and others still, stood around with drawn guns and bows. As we were now consulting in reference to the proper course to be pursued, under these peculiar and critical circumstances, their repeated demands to dismount, and their increasing determination and violence, forcibly reminded us of the eminent importance of immediate and decisive action. Finally, we determined to effect our escape, after having, slain as many of our assailants as we could, which, perhaps, might have been five of the seven, as we, together, had that number of shots, upon which we might rely. Just, however, as we had arrived at the above determination, to our astonishment, we beheld the whole country, as far as we could see, completely covered with them, rapidly advancing towards us, with deafening whoops and terrific yells. They seemed to have sprung up from behind every rock, to have come down from every hill, and mountain; and to have emerged from every valley and ravine. Our purpose was now, of course, changed, for resistance was out of the question; to attempt an escape by flight, was dangerous in the extreme, and to accomplish it was utterly impossible; we, therefore, dismounted, and determined to reconcile our minds to our fate, be that life or death. Every thing around us, appeared now, to indicate nothing but immediate torture, and ultimate death, to be inflicted by merciless savages. Their numbers had, by this time, increased to about two or three hundred; and they were still arriving in great numbers.

Rude Treatment

We were treated with the utmost rudeness; our guns and pistols were taken from us; when we were compelled to sit upon the ground, surrounded by a numerous guard, who performed its whole duty, not permitting us to change our positions in any manner, either to avoid danger, or to acquire comfort. From the time we were taken, every additional party that arrived, invariably offered some indignity to our persons, either by striking or attempting to strike us, with their bows, arrows or the rammers of their guns. The chief, however, protected me from this insult, for which purpose, he constantly stood or sat by me; yet he appeared unable, or unwilling to protect my companion, who was repeatedly stricken with much violence. An attempt was made even to take his life, which fortunately failed. This murderous attempt, was made by an Indian who had just arrived, on horseback, and who appeared to be much more infuriated than his predecessors in barbarity. Immediately upon his arrival, he rushed most furiously upon Mr. Lovejoy, suddenly pressing his gun against his breast, and snapping it, but as it missed fire, he was foiled in his fiendlike purpose. At this critical crisis, a number of Indians gathered around Mr. Lovejoy, evidently with a view of protecting him from further insult and danger, when unparalleled consternation and confusion prevailed. While many were most vehemently insisting upon our immediate destruction, others made the very welkin ring with their boisterous and clamorous declamations in our behalf, and no doubt Mr. Lovejoy and myself, owed our preservation entirely to their persuasive barbarous eloquence. The influence of our eloquent defenders was so great, as to induce the chief to order six of his men to fire upon him, who had thus rudely assailed my companion. They promptly obeyed the command, and had the offender not been making his escape with much rapidity, he would undoubtedly have been slain. Having galloped off about two hundred yards, he commenced a most doleful lamentation, and becoming more and more enraged, he set up a tremendous howling and crying, at the same time, discharging his gun in the open air; thus indicating, in terms not to be misunderstood, his determined and settled purpose of barbarous revenge. But opposition soon become so general, that he was convinced, that returning, with hostile purpose, would be attended with imminent danger. . . .

A Consultation

Some degree of quietude was again restored, but, in the meantime, my horse and Mr. Lovejoy's mule had been stripped of their saddles, bridles and martingales; all the rings and straps had been cut from them; my holster had been cut and spoiled; and our arms were scattered, we knew not where, nor was it very material where, for we had very little use for arms, and about as little for legs, as we were not permitted to stand or walk. Many were again, becoming more boisterous, when, fortunate for us, a number of elderly men, who were evidently, men of high distinction, just arrived, for whom, it appeared that the party had been thus long waiting. It was now late in the afternoon, and we were taken early in the morning; although the time of our detention, thus far, was short, it appeared long to us; hours were, to us, as days; the sun seemed reluctant to go down upon the wrath of our infuriated tormentors. A very elderly man, who was one of those that had just arrived, and who appeared to be the chief, in highest authority, after some general remarks, gave orders to march, to obey which, all were soon busily engaged in making their arrangements. Horses were provided for us, but not our own; and soon many of the party were on their march, but in the opposite direction from our company. The old chief, just referred to, happened, at this time, to pass near me, when I extended my hand to him, and accosted him in the ordinary manner, "How do you do?" He readily accepted my hand, and replied in the Indian language. There was a very small eccentric looking man, with the chief, whom I supposed to be a Canadian half-breed. I also offered him my hand, with the same salutation, to which he replied, in the English language, "How do you do?" To my inquiry whether he could speak the English language, he replied "yes." I then asked him if he would request the chief, and all those men to stop, and tell them that I wished to talk with them, before they went farther. He again replied "yes," and briefly addressed the chief, who commenced a loud harangue, to his men, and soon, those who had commenced their march returned, when all dismounted; and sitting upon the ground, side by side, formed a vast circle. The chief indicated by signs, that I and my companion, should sit near him, which we did, when I informed them that we were from the United States; that, we were sent by our and their "great father," the president, that we were going to the "great waters," the Pacific, there to settle and remain; that we were friendly with all the "red men," and that we wished to, and would treat them kindly. It had been reported among them, by some Canadians, at Fort Larimie, that we were going to join their enemies, the Black-feet, with whom they were then at war. This, I remarked, they must be satisfied, was false, especially as we had our women and children with us, of which they were aware, as they had seen them, at Fort Larimie and else-

The Trail of Tears

As settlers pushed into the Midwest, the Native American tribes of the east were being "removed" by the government to land west of the Mississippi. Fourteen thousand Cherokees were captured by General Winfield Scott in 1838 and brought to the border of Tennessee. From Tennessee they would march to reservations in the west. Four thousand died on this terrible march and became know as the Trail of Tears. By 1840 almost all of the eastern tribes had been pushed west across the Mississippi to make room for new settlers. William Coodey witnessed the first of these marches. In a letter to a friend, Coodey describes what he saw as the Indians broke camp, and the eighty-year-old chief, Going Snake, mounted his horse and led his tribe westward.

The first of September was fixed as the time for a part [of the Cherokee encampment] to be in motion on the route. Much anxiety was felt, and great exertions made by the Cherokees to comply with everything reasonably to be expected of them, and it was determined that the first detachment would move in the last days of August.

I left the Agency on the 27th, after night, and watched the encampment above alluded to, early the following morning for the purpose of aiding in the arrangements necessary to get a portion in motion on that day—the remainder to follow the next day and come up while the first were crossing the Tennessee River, about twelve miles distant.

At noon all was in readiness for moving; the teams were stretched out in a line along the road through a heavy forest,

where. White men, I remarked, did not take their women and children when they went to war, nor did Indians. Your party, I said, is a war party, and you have no women or children, because they can not fight. I then assured them, if they would go with us, to our party, we would convince them of our friendly designs; that we would trade with them, and make them presents. . . . A much more friendly feeling was now manifest towards us; we were directed to take our po-

---

groups of persons formed about each wagon, others shaking the hand of some sick friend or relative who would be left behind. The temporary camp covered with boards and some of bark that for three summer months had been their only shelter and home, were crackling and falling under a blazing flame; the day was bright and beautiful, but a gloomy thoughtfulness was depicted in the lineaments of every face. In all the bustle of preparation there was a silence and stillness of the voice that betrayed the sadness of the heart.

At length the word was given to "move on." I glanced along the line and the form of Going Snake, an aged and respected chief whose head eighty winters had whitened, mounted on his favorite pony passed before me and led the way in advance, followed by a number of young men on horse back.

At this very moment a low sound of distant thunder fell on my ear. In almost an exact western direction a dark spiral cloud was rising above the horizon and sent forth a murmur I almost fancied a voice of divine indignation for the wrongs of my poor and unhappy countrymen, driven by brutal power from all they loved and cherished in the land of their fathers, to gratify the cravings of avarice. The sun was unclouded— no rain fell—the thunder rolled away and sounds hushed in the distance. The scene around and before me, and in the elements above, were peculiarly impressive & singular. It was at once spoken of by several persons near me, and looked upon as omens of some future event in the west.

John Ehle, *The Trail of Tears: Rise and Fall of the Cherokee Nation.* New York: Doubleday, 1988.

sitions in the ranks, at the side of the chief. We soon crossed a small creek, when I indicated to the chief, by pointing to the water, then putting my fingers to my lips, that I was thirsty; upon observing which, he directed a man to dismount, and bring me some water, which direction was readily obeyed. Upon arriving with the water, the man first offered it to the chief, who refused to take it, but directed him to give it to me; which he did, when I drank and returned him the cup, which he again offered to the chief, who again refused it, directing him to give it to Mr. Lovejoy, who having drunk, the chief then received it and drank. We now traveled on with much rapidity, the "pipe of peace," being constantly passed around, commencing with the chief, then to myself, Mr. Lovejoy, and the principal men, who were permitted to ride side by side with us, and who, I suppose, were subordinate officers.

Discovery by Spies

Having traveled in this manner, about two hours, the spies came galloping from the hills, informing the chief that they had made some discoveries, which, whatever they were, were of such importance, that the chief, at once, ordered them all to dismount, which they did; and commenced examining their guns, re-loading those which had been discharged; examining their flints and locks, and putting their bows, arrows, spears and lances in proper order. Our guns were then given to us, and we were required to re-load them; when all painted their faces and bodies, as is their practice previous to going to war; after which we were all ordered to remount, and march, which we did; but, we marched with much more confusion and disorder than before. The whole aspect of things, appeared to have undergone a material and fearful change; from harmonious, peaceable and friendly, to the most tumultuous and hostile. Although we were permitted to ride, side by side, with the chief, as before, yet, I frequently saw the Indians approach Mr. Lovejoy, from behind, with drawn spears, lances, or guns, as if with a view of terminating his existence. And Mr. Lovejoy informed me, that he observed the same conduct in reference to myself, of which, however, I had no knowledge. I here saw, for the first time, that what the spies had discovered, was our company, the tents and wagons of which were then in full view. It appeared evident to us, from what we had already seen and what was then transpiring, that they contemplated an attack upon our party, and we were soon confirmed in this opinion, from what subsequently followed. When they had approached within two or three hundred rods of our camp, the young men, on each side of the chief, commenced a most furious charge, and, at the same time, uttering the most alarming and frantic yells, which left no further doubt upon our minds, but that they intended to attack our camp; unless turned from their purpose, by some fortuitous circumstance. Perceiving the inevitable tendency of this course, I suggested to the chief, by signs, that he should require his men to discontinue their charge; but he was deaf to my suggestion. I then took hold of his bridle, stopped his horse, and insisted that they must stop, otherwise, our men would be compelled to repel the assault. Being, by this time, satisfied that there was, perhaps, more danger than he had anticipated, he addressed his men in a most animated manner, apparently directing them to resume their former friendly attitude, or at least, to discontinue their charge. This order was finally obeyed, though evidently, with much reluctance. Observing that our men were in the most confused state of excitement, I signified to the chief, that I would go to our camp, to which, however, he refused his assent; but being determined to attempt it, at all hazards, I disregarded his dissent, and galloped away. Two young warriors, soon came galloping up by my side, insisting that I should return; but I answer them merely by telling them, by signs, that they must go back, or our men would shoot and kill them. This had the desired effect: they returned, and I increased my velocity, in the direction of our company. Upon arriving at the camp, I found the greatest imaginable confusion prevailing; some insisting that they would fire, others opposing it: all was noisy, alarming disorder.

Demands on the Chief

Mr. Lovejoy now having also arrived in camp, and order having been, to some extent, restored, I proceeded, through our Canadian interpreter, to make certain demands upon the chief. The first demand was, that he, immediately, send to our camp, my horse, and all other property which his men had kept, which belonged either to Mr. Lovejoy or myself. This demand he readily complied with, as far as he was able; for, as he said, he could find but one of my pistols, which he returned, together with everything else which his men had taken, with the exception of Mr. Lovejoy's bridle and martingale, which he pretended were beyond his reach, and not to be found. I then demanded, that he march his men away to a certain point of timber, and encamp during the night; to comply with which, he, at first, positively refused, insisting that an old chief, in his own country, had a right to encamp wherever he pleased; but he finally consented, when I informed him that when he had encamped, as directed, he would be permitted to return, with his chiefs and principal men; and smoke, with us, the "pipe of peace," when we would trade with them, and make him some presents. Of course, he, with several of his principal men, soon returned, much more anxious, however, to receive the promised presents, than to enter into the contemplated peace arrangements. Having formed a vast circle, all sitting upon the ground, side by side, the "pipe of peace" was soon called into requisition, which was most industriously passed and re-passed from "white chief["] to "red chief," and from "white brave" to "red brave," until we had burned several ounces of smoking tobacco, upon the altar of peace; the dense fumes of which, were curling thickly in the atmosphere above; appeasing the wrath of the "god of war," dispelling native animosity; and restoring mutual confidence, friendship and peace. After having concluded our "smoke," we traded some with them, and gave them some presents, when they left us apparently with all good feeling. . . .

From this encampment we traveled a few days up Sweetwater, where we encamped for the purpose of "making meat," as it is called. Here, while some were engaged in hunting the buffalo, which were very abundant, others remained in camp, for the purpose of protecting it, and drying and preserving the meat, which was daily brought in by the hunters. While we remained at this place, there was another accidental discharge of a gun, which produced much alarm, especially among the ladies, yet no injury resulted from it, other than a slight flesh wound in the foot, of a small child, who was sitting in a wagon, through which the ball passed. At this encampment, the Indians again, exhibited many indications of their hostile intentions. The small hunting parties, which were sent out for the purpose of hunting the buffalo, were not infrequently robbed of both their meat and horses, and sent to camp on foot, happy in having made so fortunate an escape. And they not only frequently robbed the hunters, but they also came to us in great numbers; riding and parading around our camp, insisting upon being permitted to mingle with us, which, however, I absolutely refused. . . .

Smoke and Talk

Leaving this encampment, we saw nothing more of them, for several days; but coming again, upon a tributary of Sweetwater, we met with them, in increased numbers. They numbered, at this place, not less, perhaps, than one thousand or fifteen hundred. Their numbers being now, so increased, and it being, unknown whether they were hostile, I thought proper to encamp, for the purpose of receiving and disposing of them, as circumstances might require. Accordingly, we encamped, when they advanced with much rapidity, and with most furious whoops and yells, displaying, at the same time, their flags of most beautiful and variegated colors. I now, gave them the signal to stop, which they promptly obeyed, dismounted, and planted their flag-staffs; exhibiting their colors to the best possible advantage. They were now arrayed, fronting our camp, at least, fifty abreast, and ten or twelve deep; and our greatest anxiety, of course, was to ascertain whether they were peaceably inclined; for which purpose, my horse having been saddled, I mounted and galloped out to them, when I informed them, that we would "talk" with them a few minutes, "smoke" with them, and give them some presents, when we were desirous of continuing our journey. The chiefs having manifested their approbation of this course, I invited them to our camp, to "talk" and "smoke" with us, and receive the presents, when we would all disperse. They accepted the invitation, and started with us to our camp; but as we started, the main body of the Indians also started to go with us, to have permitted which, would have been dangerous in the extreme; I, therefore, remarked to the chiefs, that the invitation, was only extended to them, and that, we would expect the residue of the Indians, to remain where they were, as much confusion, and perhaps, difficulty, might result from their intermingling with our people. They replied through their interpreter, in their brief manner, "it is good," "it is right." Then turning to their men, they gave them orders to remain, until they should return. We then proceeded to our "talk," and "smoke," which engaged our attention about two hours; when we distributed the promised presents among them, took our leave of them, and pursued our journey; while they returned to their villages, with the kindest feelings and warmest friendship, for the "white man of the East." As we passed their villages, which were but a few hundred yards from our route, hundreds of the women and children thronged our way, gazing upon us with the utmost astonishment; and many of the men followed us, even until night, when, after having effected many profitable trades in horses and mules, they returned to their villages, rejoicing in the happy anticipation, of the extraordinary advantages, to be derived from their new acquaintances, thus favorably formed.

Trading with the Utah

Edwin Bryant

Edwin Bryant was born in Massachusetts in 1805. He moved
with his family to Kentucky in 1816 and became a newspaper
editor with the Louisville *Courier-Journal*. He decided to
travel west for health reasons and set out with two friends,
Richard Jacob and Robert Ewing, in 1846. Bryant initially
joined a large wagon train company, but later he and his
friends sold their wagons and continued by mule train. He
arrived at Fort Bridger in Wyoming on July 16 where he actually met Lansford W. Hastings who was trying to convince
pioneers to settle in California.

Part of the purpose of Bryant's journey was to write a book
on his adventures. In 1847 he completed *What I Saw in California*. When it was published in 1848, it caught the enormous public interest in the gold rush and became very popular both in America and in Europe. In this account, Bryant
reports on an encounter with the Utah Indians. He attempted
to trade for some meat, but the Indians had none. In exchange
for some darning needles the Indians gave him what was
known as "fruit cake"—a dried mixture of berries and
grasshoppers. Bryant made the trade near the Great Salt Lake
and included the incident in his popular book.

July 30.—At sunrise, clear and calm, with an agreeable
temperature. The morning scene was beautifully grand.
Our camp being in the shadow of the mountains, the face of

Excerpted from *What I Saw in California*, by Edwin Bryant (Lincoln: University of Nebraska Press, 1985).

the sun was invisible to us, long after his golden rays had tipped, one after another, the summits of the far-distant islands in the lake. By degrees the vast expanse of waters became illuminated, reflecting the bright beams of the god of day with dazzling effulgence.

Our route to-day continued south, near the base of the range of mountains on our left. We frequently crossed deep ravines and piles of granite debris, with which the slope of the mountains in places is covered. Travelling about ten miles we reached the southern extremity of one of the bays of the Salt Lake [Farmington Bay]. Beyond this there is a basin of water some three or four miles in circumference, surrounded by a smooth sandy beach. An immense number of ducks were walking and flying over this beach and playing in the basin. Approaching the shore of the pond, a solitary Indian rose from the weeds or grass near the water, and discovering us, he started immediately and ran with considerable speed towards a point of the mountains on our left. Several of us pursued and overtook him. He appeared much alarmed at first, but after shaking hands with us, and discovering that we had no hostile intentions, he soon forgot his fright. He carried in his hand a miserably lean duck, which he had just killed with an arrow. A quiver slung across his bare and tawny shoulders, was well supplied with this weapon. He was naked, with the exception of a small covering around his loins, and his skin was as dark as a dark mulatto. Learning from him that he was a Utah, we endeavored to make him comprehend that we wished to trade with his tribe for elk-meat. He shook his head, and appearing desirous of leaving us, we dismissed him. He was soon out of sight, hurrying away with long and rapid strides.

Proceeding about two miles and turning the point of the mountain, we came to seven warm springs, so strongly impregnated with sulphur as to have left a deposite of this mineral in some places several feet in depth. These springs gush out near the foot of a high precipice, composed of conglomerate rock and a bluish sandstone. The precipice seems to have been uplifted by some subterraneous convulsion.

The temperature of the water in the basins was about 90°. The water of most of them was bitter and nauseous.

From these springs we crossed a level plain, on which we encamped at 11 o'clock, A.M., near a small stream of cold water [City Creek] flowing from the mountains, which is skirted with a few poplars and small willows. The grass immediately around our camp is fresh and green, but a short distance from us it is brown, dry, and crisp.

Visited by Indians

After dinner we were visited by three Indians, one of whom was the man with the duck we saw this morning. The eldest of the three signified that he wished a friendly smoke and a "talk." A pipe was produced and filled with tobacco. Lighting it, I drew two or three puffs and handed it to the old man, and it passed from him to his comrades until the tobacco was consumed. They appeared to enjoy the fumes of the smoke highly. We informed them of our wish to trade for meat. They signified that they had none. Three females of middle age, miserably clad and ugly, soon made their appearance, bringing baskets containing a substance, which, upon examination, we ascertained to be service-berries, crushed to a *jam* and mixed with pulverized grasshoppers. This composition being dried in the sun until it becomes hard, is what may be called the "fruit-cake" of these poor children of the desert. No doubt these women regarded it as one of the most acceptable offerings they could make to us. We purchased all they brought with them, paying them in darning-needles and other small articles, with which they were much pleased. The prejudice against the grasshopper "fruit-cake" was strong at first, but it soon wore off, and none of the delicacy was thrown away or lost.

Two of our party mounted their mules and rode to the Indian encampment to ascertain if there were not more Indians, and some from whom meat could be obtained. As soon as the men and women in our camp saw them riding in the direction of their lodges, they hastened away with great speed and in much alarm. Returning from the Indian encampment, Jacob and Brookey reported that there were no more Indians, and that no meat could be obtained. They saw a large quantity of grasshoppers, or crickets, (the insect I have before described,) which were being prepared for pulverization.

The Indians of this region, in order to capture this insect with greater facility, dig a pit in the ground. They then make what hunters, for brevity of expression, call a *surround*;— that is, they form a circle at a distance around this pit, and drive the grass-hoppers or crickets into it, when they are easily secured and taken. After being killed, they are baked before the fire or dried in the sun, and then pulverized between smooth stones. Prejudice aside, I have tasted what are called delicacies, less agreeable to the palate. Although the Utahs are a powerful and warlike tribe, these Indians appeared to be wretchedly destitute. . . .

Utah Outlet

July 31.—Morning clear, with a delightful temperature, and a light breeze blowing from the west. Our route to-day runs in a west course across the valley of the "Utah Outlet" [Jordan River], about ten miles south from the bay or arm of the Salt Lake upon which we have been travelling. The waters of the Utah Lake are emptied into the Salt Lake through this channel. The Utah Lake is a body of fresh water between sixty and eighty miles in circumference, situated about twenty miles south of the Salt Lake. The shape of the extensive plain of this lake was made apparent to us by the mountains surrounding it. The plain of the lake is said to be fertile, but of the extent of its fertility I have no certain knowledge. The eastern side of the valley of the "Outlet" is well watered by small streams running from the mountains, and the grass and other herbage on the upland are abundant, but there is no timber visible from our position. . . .

Our route for several hours described nearly a semicircle, when there was a break in the range of mountains, and we entered upon another plain [Tooele Valley]. About three o'clock, P.M., we passed several remarkable rocks rising in tower-like shapes from the plain, to the height of sixty or eighty feet. Beyond these we crossed two small streams bitter with saline and alkaline impregnation. The plain presents a sterile appearance, but little vegetation appearing upon it, and that stunted and withered. At seven o'clock, P.M., we reached a spring branch descending from a mountain ravine, and fringed with small willows, the water of which is comparatively fresh and cool. Here we encamped after a march without halting, of twelve hours. There is a variety of vegetation along the stream—grass, weeds, some few flowers, briers, and rose-bushes.

Utah Vocabulary

Soon after we encamped, three Utah Indians visited us. They were mounted on horses, rather lean, and sore-backed from hard usage. The men appeared to be of a better class and more intelligent than those we had before met with. They were young and manifested much sprightliness, and an inquisitive curiosity, which they took no pains to conceal. We invited them to sup with us, and they partook of our simple viands with a high relish. A renewal of our overtures to trade for meat met with no better success than before. They had no meat to dispose of. They were dressed in buckskin shirts, gaiters, and moccasins; and armed with bows and arrows. Two of these men, the most intelligent, concluded to encamp with us for the night. The principal of these, a young man of about twenty-five, with an amiable but sprightly expression of countenance, was so earnest and eager in his inquiries respecting every thing appertaining to us, and into our language, that I sat conversing with him until a late hour of the night. From him I learned the names of many things in the Utah dialect. I give some of these below. The orthography is in strict accordance with the sound.

ENGLISH.	UTAH.	ENGLISH.	UTAH.
Tobacco	Pah.	Water	Poh.
Fire	Coutouch.	Eye	Pooh.
Grass	Shawnip.	Ear	Nank.
Hair	Pamp.	Nose	Tamoucher.

Sun	Tarp.	Hand	Moh.
Powder-horn	Naup.	Flint	Tuck.
Spur	Tannegan.	Wood	Schnip.
Mule	Moodah.	Blanket	Tochewanup.
Bullet	Navak.	Pipe	Toh.
Knife	Weitch.	Teeth	Tamp.
Horse	Punk.	Bear	Padewap.
Finger	Mushevan.	Rifle	Wokeat.
Foot	Mamp.	Powder	Noketouch.
Bear's Claw	Musheta.	Pantaloons	Wannacouch.
	Middenah.	Saddle.	

These are some of the words of the Utah language which I wrote down, from his pronunciations, by the light of our campfire. Furnishing him and his companion some skins, we requested them to retire for the night, which they seemed to do with reluctance. Distance 40 miles.

The Nine-Shooter Incident

August 1.—Morning clear, with a delightfully soft breeze from the south. I purchased, this morning, of one of the Utahs, a dressed grisly bear-skin, for which I gave him twenty charges of powder and twenty bullets. Several other small trades were made with them by our party. Having determined to cross a range of mountains, instead of following to avoid it, the shore of another cove or bay of the Salt Lake,—by doing which we should lose in distance twenty-five or thirty miles,—we laid our course nearly west, towards the lowest gap we could discover in the range.

After we had proceeded two or three miles up the sloping plain, towards the base of the mountains, Colonel Russell recollected that he had left his rifle at the camp—a "nine-shooter." Accompanied by Miller, he returned back to recover it. I was very well satisfied that the Indians would have discovered it, and considering it a valuable prize, would not wait for the return of the loser. According to their code of morals, it is not dishonest to take what is left in camp, and they never fail to do it. I halted for an hour, and long after our party had disappeared in a gorge of the mountains, for the return of Colonel Russell and Miller. I could see, from my elevated position, the dust raised by the horses of the retreating Indians on the plain, at a distance of six or eight miles from the camp. Becoming impatient, I commenced a countermarch, and while moving on, I saw, at a distance of a mile and a half, a solitary horseman, urging his animal with great speed towards me. There being but one instead of two, I felt considerable anxiety, not knowing but some disaster might have occurred. I moved faster towards the horseman, and, at the distance of a quarter of a mile, discovered that it was Colonel Russell. Riding towards him, I inquired what had become of Miller? He did not know. He had lost him in hunting through the willows and ravines. My anxiety was much increased at this report, and I started to return to the camp, when Miller, proceeding at a slow gait, appeared on one of the distant elevations. The result of the search for the "nine-shooting" rifle was fruitless. The Indians had carried it away with them. The only consolation I could offer to Colonel Russell for his loss was, that a more useless burden was never carried on the shoulders of man or mule. It was a weight upon the beast, and an incumbrance to the rider, and of no practical utility on this journey. This consolation, however, was not very soothing.

(I will state here, that this rifle was recovered by Mr. Hudspeth, brought into California, and returned to Colonel Russell. The Indian who took it from our camp, after he had returned to the village of his tribe, was much elated by his prize. But in discharging it, the ball, instead of making its passage through the barrel, took another direction, and wounded him in the leg. An instrument so mysterious and eccentric it was considered dangerous to retain, and the chief ordered its restoration to the emigrant parties following us. It was recognized by Mr. Hudspeth, and returned to its owner, as above stated.)

Captivity Among the Sioux

Fanny Kelly

Fanny Kelly had grown up in eastern Kansas and married a local farmer, Josiah. Because of a severe drought in 1860, a grasshopper plague the next year, and border conflicts in the Civil War, the Kellys decided to move west in 1864. They brought with them a good supply of trade goods: flour, coffee, dried and canned fruit, whiskey, brandy, and a herd of fifty milk cows and twenty-five calves worth $15,200. They traveled in a small party with seven men, two women and two children including their eight-year-old, adopted daughter, Mary. Fanny was optimistic about her family's prospects for a new life in California.

Shortly after passing Chimney Rock and Scott's Bluff in Nebraska, they met a band of Sioux. The Indians traveled with them for an hour and then attacked without warning. The Sioux killed three men, wounded two and captured Fanny and her daughter Mary. In minutes, Fanny's hope for a better life was utterly shattered.

The Indians took captives, both white and Indian, as a valuable prize. Sometimes the captives became helpers and part of the tribe—not quite slaves. Some were traded to other tribes or to white men for horses, guns, and liquor. Although these kidnappings were not common, they did occur and had been occurring since the first colonists landed in the New World.

Fanny and her Sioux captors traveled almost four hundred miles in thirteen days back to their village in the north part of what would become South Dakota. On the first day, Fanny

Excerpted from *Narrative of My Captivity Among the Sioux Indians*, by Fanny Kelly (Chicago: R.R. Donnelley & Sons Company, 1990).

managed to hide her daughter Mary in the bushes and told her to find her way back to the trail. Her husband, Josiah, who survived the attack, later found Mary dead, shot with arrows and scalped. Fanny spent several months with the Sioux and then was returned to Fort Skully as part of the tribe's peace settlement with the government. She later wrote a best-selling book about her captivity.

Truly, those pictures of the children of the forest that adorn the pages of the novelist are delightful conceptions of the airy fancy, fitted to charm the mind. They amuse and beguile the hours they invest with their interest; . . . the true red man, as I saw him, does not exist between the pages of many volumes. He roams his native wastes, and to once encounter and study him there, so much must be sacrificed that I was unable to appreciate the knowledge I was gaining at such a price.

Notwithstanding all I had seen and experienced, I do recall much that was gentle and faithful in the character associated with the Indian women. Perhaps I might be able to find one whose sympathy and companionship could be wrought upon to the extent of aiding me in some way to escape. I became hopeful with the thought, and almost forgot my terror of the threats of my captors in my desire to see the friendly faces of Indian women.

The country around was rich and varied. Beautiful birds appeared in the trees and flowers of variety and fragrance nodded on their stems. Wild fruits were abundant and I plucked roses and fruit for food, while my savage companions feasted on raw meat. They did not seem to care for fruit, and urged me to eat meat with them. I refused because of its being raw. A young Indian, guessing the cause of my refusal to eat, procured a kettle, made a fire, cooked some, and offered it to me. I tried to eat of it to please them, since they had taken the trouble to prepare a special dish, but owing to the filthy manner in which it was prepared, a very small portion satisfied me.

We were now nearing a river, which, from its locality,

must have been the Tongue River, where we found refreshing drink, and rested for a short time. The Indians gave me to understand that when we crossed this stream, and a short distance beyond, we would be at their home.

Grand Entrance

Here they paused to dress, so as to make a gay appearance and imposing entrance into the village. Except when in full dress, an Indian's wearing apparel consists only of a buffalo robe, which is also part of a fine toilet. It is quite inconveniently disposed about the person, without any fastening, and must be held in position with the hands.

Here the clothing seized from our train was brought into great demand, and each warrior that had been fortunate enough to possess himself of any article of our dress, now arrayed himself to the best advantage the garments and their limited ideas of civilization would permit. In several instances when the toilet was considered complete, changes for less attractive articles of display were made with companions who had not been so fortunate as others in the division of the goods, that they might also share in the sport afforded by this derisive display.

Their peculiar ideas of tasteful dress rendered them grotesque in appearance. One darkened face appeared under the shade of my hat, smiling with obvious satisfaction at the superiority of his decorations over those of his less fortunate companions; another was shaded from the scorching rays of the sun by a tiny parasol, and the brown hand that held it aloft was thinly covered by a silk glove, which was about the only article of clothing, except the invariable breechcloth that the warrior wore. . . .

The War Chief

Ottawa, or Silver Horn, the war chief, was arrayed in complete costume. He was quite old, over seventy-five, partially blind, and under the medium height. He was ferocious and savage looking, and now, when in costume, looked frightful. His face was red with stripes of black, and around each eye a circlet of bright yellow. His long, black hair was divided into two braids with a scalp lock on top of the head. His ears held great brass wire rings, six full inches in diameter, and chains and beaded necklaces were suspended from his neck. Armlets and bracelets of brass, together with a string of bears' claws, completed his jewelry. He also wore leggings of deer skin, and a shirt of the same material, beautifully ornamented with beads, and fringed with scalp locks, which he claimed to have been taken from his enemies, both red and white. Across his shoulders hung a great, bright-colored quilt, that had been taken from our stores. He wore a crown of eagle feathers on his head; also a long plume of feathers descending from the back of the crown.

His horse, a noble-looking animal, was no less gorgeously arrayed. His ears were pierced, like his master's, and his neck was encircled by a wreath of bears' claws, taken from animals that the chief had slain. Some bells and a human scalp hung from his mane, forming together, thus arrayed, a museum of the trophies of the old chief's prowess on the warpath, and of skill in the chase.

When all was arranged, the chief mounted his horse and rode on in triumph toward the village, highly elated over the possession of his white captive, whom he never looked back at or deigned to notice, except to chastise on account of her slowness, which was unavoidable, as I rode a jaded horse and could not keep pace.

The Indian Village

The entire Indian village poured forth to meet us, amid song and wild dancing in the most enthusiastic manner; flourishing flags and weapons of war in frenzied joy as we entered the village, which, stretched for miles along the banks of the stream. It resembled a vast military encampment, with the wigwams covered with white skins, like Sibley tents in shape and size, ranged without regard to order, but facing one point of the compass.

We penetrated through the irregular settlement for over a

mile, accompanied by the enthusiastic escort of men, women, and children.

I rode in the center of a double column of Indians and directly in the rear of the chief until we reached the door of his lodge, when several of his wives came out to meet him. He had six, but the senior one remained in the tent, while a younger one was absent with the Farmer or Grosventre Indians. Their salutation is very much in the manner of the Mexicans; the women crossed their arms on the chief's breast, and smiled.

They met me in silence, but with looks of great astonishment.

I got down as directed, and followed the chief into the great lodge or tent, distinguished from the others by its superior ornaments. It was decorated with brilliantly colored porcupine quills and a terrible fringe of human scalp locks, the results of several battles with the Pawnees.

On one side was depicted a representation of the Good Spirit, rude in design and daubed with colors. On the other side was portrayed the figure of the spirit of evil in like manner. The Indians believe in these two deities and pay their homage to them. The first they consider to be entirely benevolent and kind, but the second is filled with vile tricks and wicked ways.

They fear him and consider it only safe to propitiate him occasionally by obedience to his evil will. This may account for some of their worst ferocities and explain that horrible brutality of nature which they so often exhibit.

The senior wife, who had remained in the lodge, met her husband with the same salutation as the others had done.

I was shown to a seat on a buffalo skin opposite the entrance. The chief's spoil was brought in for division by his elderly spouse.

As it was spread out before them, the women gathered admiringly around, and proved their peculiarities of taste. The love of finery had a counterpart in these forest belles, as well defined as if they had been city ladies. Eagerly they watched every new article displayed, grunting their approval, until their senior companion seized a piece of cloth, declaring that she meant to retain it for herself.

This occasioned dissatisfaction, which soon ripened to rebellion among them, and they contended for a just distribution of the goods. The elder matron, following her illustrious husband's plan in quelling such outbreaks, caught her knife from her belt, sprang in among them, vowing that she was the oldest and had the right to govern, and threatening to kill everyone if there was the least objection offered to her decrees. I had so hoped to find sympathy and pity among these artless women of the forest, but instead, cowed and trembling, I sat, scarcely daring to breathe.

The chief noticed my fear and shrinking posture, and smiled. Then he rose and made a speech, which had its effect. The women became quiet. Presently an invitation arrived for the chief to go to a feast, and he rose to comply.

With the Women and Children

I followed his departing figure with regret, for, terrible as he and his men had been, the women seemed still more formidable, and I feared to be left alone with them, especially because of the hot temper and ready knife of the elder squaw.

Great crowds of curious Indians came flocking in to stare at me. The women brought their children. Some of them, whose fair complexion astonished me, I afterward learned were the offspring of fort marriages.

One fair little boy who, with his mother, had just returned from Fort Laramie, came close to me. Finding the squaw could speak a few words in English, I addressed her and was told, in reply to my questions, that she had been the wife of a captain there, but because his white wife would soon be arriving from the East, his Indian wife was to return to her people. She did so, taking her child with her. The little boy was outfitted completely in military clothing, even to the stripe on his pantaloons. He appeared to be a very bright, attractive child of about four years.

It was a very sad thought for me to realize that a parent could part with such a child, committing it forever to live in barbarous ignorance, and rove the woods among savages with the impress of his own superior race, so strongly mingled with his Indian origin. I saw many other fair-faced little children, and heard the sad story from their mothers, and was deeply pained to see their pale, pinched features as they cried for food when there was none to be had. On many occasions they are cruelly treated by the full-blooded and larger children because of their unfortunate birth.

As soon as the question of property was decided between the women of the chief's family, they became more kindly disposed toward me, and one of them brought me a dish of meat. Many others followed her example, even those from the neighboring lodges. All really seemed to pity me, and showed great evidences of compassion. They tried to express their sympathy in signs, because I had been torn from my own people and compelled to come on such a long, fatiguing journey. They examined me over and over again, particularly my dress, hands, and feet. Then, to their great surprise, they discovered my bruised and almost broken limbs that occurred when first taken, also from the fall of the horse the first night of my captivity, and proceeded at once to dress my wounds.

The Chief's Summons

I was just beginning to rejoice in the dawning kindness that seemed to soften their swarthy faces when a messenger from the war chief arrived, accompanied by a small party of young warriors sent to conduct me to the chief's presence. I did not at first comprehend the summons, and, as every fresh announcement only awakened new fears, I dreaded to comply, yet dared not refuse. Seeing my hesitation, the senior wife allowed a little daughter of the chief's, whose name was Yellow Bird, to accompany me, and I was then conducted to several feasts, at each of which I was received with kindness, and promised good will and protection. It was here that the chief himself first condescended to talk kindly to me, and this and the companionship of the child, Yellow Bird, who seemed to approach me with a trusting grace and freedom unlike the scared shyness of Indian children generally, inspired hope.

The chief here told me that henceforth I could call Yellow Bird my own, to take the place of my little girl that had been killed. I did not at once comprehend all of his meaning, still it gave me some hope of security.

At nightfall, after we came back to the lodge, which they told me I must henceforth regard as home, I found the elder women busily pounding a post into the ground, and my fears were at once aroused. I was always ready to become afraid when something suggested a token of some evil. On the contrary, it was simply some household arrangement of her own, for presently, putting on a camp kettle, she built a fire and caused water to boil, and drew a tea of which she gave me a portion, assuring me that it would cure the tired and weary feeling and secure me a good rest. . . .

Before my eyes closed in slumber my heart rose in gratitude unspeakable to God for his great and immeasurable mercy.

I readily adapted myself to my new position. The chief's three sisters shared the lodge with us.

The following day commenced my labors, and the chief's wife seemed to feel a protecting interest in me.

The Dog Feast

The day of the twenty-fifth of July was observed by continual feasting in honor of the safe return of the braves.

There was a large tent made by putting several together, where all the chiefs, medicine men, and great warriors met for consultation and feasting. I was invited to attend, and was given an elevated seat, while the rest of the company all sat cross-legged upon the ground preparatory to the feast being dealt out.

In the center of the circle was erected a flagstaff with many scalps, trophies, and ornaments fastened to it. Near the foot of the flagstaff were placed, in a row on the ground, several large kettles in which was prepared the feast. Also, on the ground near the kettles, was a bevy of wooden bowls in which the meat was to be served. In front there were two or three women, who were acting as waiters to light the pipes for smoking as well as to serve the food. While I remained seated, thousands began climbing and crowding around for a peep at me. At length, the chief arose in a very handsome costume, and addressed the audience. I could understand but little of his meaning, but he often pointed to me.

Several others also made speeches that sounded the same to me. I sat trembling with fear at these strange proceedings, fearing they were deliberating upon a plan of putting me to some cruel death to finish their amusement. It is impossible to describe my feelings on that day, as I sat in the midst of those wild, savage people. Soon a handsome pipe was lit and brought to the chief to smoke. He took it, and after presenting the stem to the north, the south, the east, and the west, and then to the sun that was over his head, uttered a few words, drew a few whiffs, then passed it around through the whole group, who all smoked. This smoking was conducted with the strictest adherence to exact and established form, and the entire feast was conducted in the most positive silence.

The lids were raised from the kettles, which were all filled with dog's meat that had been well cooked and made into some sort of stew. Each guest had a large wooden bowl placed before him with a quantity of dog's flesh enmeshed in a profusion of soup or rich gravy. A large spoon, made of buffalo horn, rested in the dish.

In this most difficult and painful dilemma I sat witnessing the solemnity; my dish was given to me, and the absolute necessity of eating it was painful to contemplate. I tasted it a few times after much urging, and then resigned my dish, which was taken and passed around with others to every part of the group, who all ate heartily. In this way the feast ended, and all retired silently and gradually until the ground was left to the waiters. . . .

As far as I could see and understand, I feel authorized to pronounce the dog-feast a truly religious ceremony, wherein the superstitious Indian sees fit to sacrifice his faithful companion to bear testimony to the sacredness of his vows of friendship for the Great Spirit. He first offers a portion of meat to his deity, then places it on the ground to remind him of the sacrifice and solemnity of the offering. . . .

Their village was well supplied with fresh and dried meat of the buffalo and deer. The dog-feast is given, I believe, by all tribes in America, and in them all this faithful animal, as well as the horse, is sacrificed in several different ways to appease offended spirits or deities, whom it is considered necessary that they should conciliate in this way. This is invariably done by giving the best in the herd or the kennel.

That night was spent in dancing. It seemed quite wild and furious to me. I was led into the center of the circle, and assigned the painful duty of holding above my head human scalps fastened to a little pole. The dance was kept up until near morning, when all repaired to their respective lodges. The three kind sisters of the chief were there to convey me to mine.

Chapter 5

Homesteading

Chapter Preface

O nce the hardships of the journey were over, the pioneers began to establish their new lives. One of the most important things they had to do was quickly claim land for themselves. The Homestead Act of 1862 provided them with 160 acres of land for the fee of ten dollars. In some areas, the wife was also allowed to claim an additional 160 acres. Next, they had to build their log cabins and sod houses. "Weeks of hard labor were required to fell trees, clear away the brush and prepare the site," said Charlotte Cartwright, who settled in Oregon in 1845. They often had to live in their wagons until suitable housing could be constructed. The greatest challenge was to survive through the first winter. They were isolated in the wilderness and often felt homesick. Cut off from civilization, they had to rely on themselves and on their own hard work to live off the land they had claimed.

On the plains, the pioneers' first home might be a house made from prairie sod. Door and window frames were made from wood, as was the roof. The roof was also covered with a layer of sod. Inside, the house was always dark. When it rained, mud dripped from the ceiling. The furniture was crude and homemade. The houses had fireplaces, but wood was scarce on the prairie, and corncobs were often used to cook meals in an iron stove.

The pioneers had to produce almost all of the necessities of life. They had to build furniture and make their own clothing. In some areas, such as Oregon, cotton and wool were not available. The nearest store was thirty miles or more away. And if they got to a store, the goods were either very expensive or the shopkeeper might not have what was needed. But the pioneers were very self-reliant. They made soap from animal fat, created dye from tree bark, brewed tea from wild herbs, and boiled carrots with sugar to make jam.

After the first crops were planted, the pioneers faced other problems. The plains were plagued by swarms of crickets that could consume a field of wheat overnight. A lack of rainfall and droughts were also problems on the plains. Dams and irrigation canals had to be built. Some settlers lost their crops when they had to flee from wars with the Indians. Others lost their entire homestead in legal disputes over the claim to their land. The pioneers had made a long, arduous journey in search of a new home, but that idealized way of life was not going to come easy.

Appraising the Frontiersmen

Timothy Flint

Timothy Flint was a New Englander and a Harvard graduate. After his graduation he became a Congregational minister and preached for twelve years before becoming a missionary in the Mississippi Valley. He was outspoken and blunt in his sermons, more concerned with practical issues than theology. He was often involved in controversy with his church members and sometimes had a hard time collecting his salary of four hundred dollars a year. When he lost his minister position he decided to move west and become a missionary. Flint traveled constantly for ten years up and down the Mississippi Valley from St. Louis to New Orleans from 1815 to 1825. His book, *Recollections of the Last Ten Years*, is one of the best studies of the American frontier of the period. While he did retain some of his New England prejudices, he had a great love of his newly adopted frontier life and the people who lived there. In this selection of his book, Flint pays tribute to the character of these settlers without idealizing or over-romanticizing them.

T he people in the Atlantic states have not yet recovered from the horror inspired by the term "backwoodsman." This prejudice is particularly strong in New England and is more or less felt from Maine to Georgia. When I first visited this country, I had my full share, and my family by far too much for their comfort. In approaching the country, I heard

Excerpted from *Recollections of the Last Ten Years*, by Timothy Flint (Carbondale: Southern Illinois University Press, 1968).

a thousand stories of gougings and robberies and shooting down with the rifle. I have traveled in these regions thousands of miles under all circumstances of exposure and danger. I have traveled alone or in company only with such as needed protection, instead of being able to impart it, and this too, in many instances, where I was not known as a minister or where such knowledge would have had no influence in protecting me. I never have carried the slightest weapon of defense. I scarcely remember to have experienced anything that resembled insult or to have felt myself in danger from the people. I have often seen men that had lost an eye. Instances of murder, numerous and horrible in their circumstances, have occurred in my vicinity. But they were such lawless encounters as terminate in murder everywhere, and in which the drunkenness, brutality, and violence were mutual. They were catastrophes in which quiet and sober men would be in no danger of being involved. When we look round these immense regions and consider that I have been in settlements three hundred miles from any court of justice, when we look at the position of the men and the state of things, the wonder is that so few outrages and murders occur. The gentlemen of the towns, even here [Louisiana], speak often with a certain contempt and horror of the backwoodsmen. It is true there are worthless people here; it is true there are gamblers and gougers and outlaws, but there are fewer of them than, from the nature of things and the character of the age and the world, we ought to expect.

To Have Plenty of Rich Land

But the backwoodsman of the west, as I have seen him, is generally an amiable and virtuous man. His general motive for coming here is to be a freeholder, to have plenty of rich land, and to be able to settle his children about him. It is a most virtuous motive. And I fully believe that nine in ten of the emigrants have come here with no other motive. You find, in truth, that he has vices and barbarisms peculiar to his situation. His manners are rough. He wears, it may be, a long beard. He has a great quantity of bear- or deerskins wrought into his household establishment, his furniture and dress. He carries a knife or a dirk in his bosom, and when in the woods has a rifle on his back and a pack of dogs at his heels. An Atlantic stranger, transferred directly from one of our cities to his door, would recoil from an encounter with him. But remember that his rifle and his dogs are among his chief means of support and profit. Remember that all his first days here were passed in dread of the savages. Remember that he still encounters them, still meets bears and panthers.

Hospitality

Enter his door and tell him you are benighted and wish the shelter of his cabin for the night. The welcome is indeed seemingly ungracious: "I reckon you can stay" or "I suppose we must let you stay." But this apparent ungraciousness is the harbinger of every kindness that he can bestow and every comfort that his cabin can afford. Good coffee, cornbread and butter, venison, pork, wild and tame fowls, are set before you. His wife, timid, silent, reserved, but constantly attentive to your comfort, does not sit at the table with you, but like the wives of the patriarchs, stands and attends on you. You are shown to the best bed which the house can afford. When this kind of hospitality has been afforded you as long as you choose to stay, and when you depart and speak about your bill, you are most commonly told with some slight mark of resentment that they do not keep tavern. Even the flaxen-headed urchins will turn away from your money. . . .

Sincere and Upright

I have found the backwoodsmen to be such as I have described—a hardy, adventurous, hospitable, rough, but sincere and upright race of people. I have received so many kindnesses from them that it becomes me always to preserve a grateful and affectionate remembrance of them. If we were to try them by the standard of New England customs and opinions, that is to say, the customs of a people under entirely different circumstances, there would be many things in the picture that would strike us offensively. They care little about ministers and think less about paying them. They are averse to all, even the most necessary, restraints. They are destitute of the forms and observances of society and religion, but they are sincere and kind without professions and have a coarse but substantial morality.

The Move onto the Kansas Prairie

Percy G. Ebbutt

This report on Kansas pioneer life in the 1870s was written
by Percy G. Ebbutt for an English audience when he returned
home to England. Ebbutt left Blaxton in the south of England
when he was ten years old. He made the trip with his brother,
father and three other young men. His father was a successful
upholsterer who decided to go to Kansas when the family's
home burned down. Of the six pioneers, only one, Will
Humphrey, had any experience with farming. They embarked
by steamer from Liverpool and crossed the "Herring Pond" as
the Atlantic Ocean was nicknamed in twelve days with nine
hundred emigrants on board. They traveled by rail to Junction
City, Kansas, and from there they hauled their luggage by
wagon onto the prairie to start their new life.

O n the 18th of February, 1871, having hired a couple of
waggons, we moved up on the prairie with all our luggage, and boards to build our house with. On arriving at our
destination, seven miles from town, the large boxes were
piled up, and the boards laid slanting from the top to the
ground for a roof, and thus we made a very comfortable
shanty. It was certainly none too large, though, for six of us,
. . . and it was so low that no one could stand upright in it at
the highest part. However, with the exception of the cook,
we did not spend much time indoors—there was no door,
though. We had an iron stove for cooking in one corner, with

Excerpted from *Emigrant Life in Kansas*, by Percy G. Ebbutt (London: Swan Sonnenschein and Co., 1886).

the flue running through the top, which once set fire to the *building*; but as we had plenty of water handy we were able to extinguish it before it did much damage. We were very well off for provisions, having a good supply of bacon, biscuits, eggs, cheese, coffee, sugar, flour, rice, etc. The cook, Harry Parker, made his first attempt at bread-baking before we had been here many days, but was not over successful. The bread was baked in a great iron pan, and was as hard as a well-done brick, and about as digestible. The outside could not be cut with a knife, we were obliged to use a hatchet to make any impression. However, a few more trials soon improved the baking. For fuel we had to go about a mile down a little creek. . . . There were some small trees growing which we chopped down and dragged up to the shanty on wheelbarrows, not having any horses as yet. . . .

Revolver Accident

While living in this mansion we had our first sight of a prairie fire, but as it was on high ground, where the grass was not rank, and there was very little wind, it was not particularly fierce. While living here we almost had an accident. We had amongst our collection an old pepper-box revolver, a stupid thing, with six barrels the full length of the machine, and not six chambers and one long barrel as usual. Well, this old thing was loaded, and some of the party, who had been practising shooting at a shingle target, were standing about trying to make the pepper-box go off, but it would not. They snapped and snapped, but without effect, until presently I took it up and pulled the trigger; it hung there for an instant, and then gave such a kick as to almost knock me over, and the bullets went flying just over the heads of my friends. All six chambers went off at once for some inscrutable reason, but fortunately no one was hurt.

Our Shanty Built on the Wrong Land

The country around had all been surveyed by Government previous to our settling, and divided into square miles,— sections, they are called,—marked with a stone set in the ground. They may then be cut up easily into the required lots—viz., eighty acres for an ordinary settler, and one hundred and sixty [acres] for any man who has been a soldier in the Federal Army. When we began to look around us, we found that our goods were all dropped upon land belonging to Parker instead of to my father, and as the house was to be built upon land belonging to the latter, all the boards, etc., had to be moved about half a mile upon the wheelbarrows. As we had a stream to cross on the way it was no easy task, but with one to push the barrow and another in front with a rope, we managed very well, getting stuck; in the mud a few times, though, when it took all the available hands to pull the vehicle out. . . .

It may seem rather a funny thing to do, to go into a house before the roof is on; but you see, as we built the house we robbed the boards which formed the top of the box shanty, so that we were bound to sleep without a roof in any case. We did all the work ourselves, having a carpenter's bench and plenty of tools, and made quite a comfortable little house. Certainly it was not very large, having only one room, fourteen feet by twelve, with an attic above, but it was large enough, especially in cold weather, and in hot weather we lived out of doors mostly. The attic was reached by a series of holes cut in the wall for hands and feet, which led to a trap-door in the ceiling, so that no room was lost by having a flight of stairs.

For a table we used the carpenter's bench, and for beds we had the large boxes ranged round the room, which also, when the blankets were rolled up, served us as seats.

Almost in the centre of the room stood the cooking stove with an iron pipe through the end of the house, so that with a row of drawers and shelves for the crockery, our room was pretty full of furniture.

"Broad" and "Pretty"

After the house was completed we had to set to work to improve the land in all ways, and horses and oxen were bought to plough with. Our first purchase was a yoke of oxen. They were not long from Texas, and not more than half broken in, and were a funny couple. To begin with, they did not at all match in colour, nor were they much alike in other respects. We called them "Broad" and "Pretty"—queer names for oxen you will say. Broad was about as fat as a slate and Pretty—well, he was not named according to his looks anyhow, nor was his temper of the best description. He was a most vicious and obstinate old brute. Broad was a decent old chap, but awfully lazy, and would let us ride on his back, being too lazy to trouble about the matter; he could easily have fetched us off with his tremendous horns.

These animals were often a fearful bother to yoke up, as you might get one in, and dodge around with the other for half an hour before getting him under the yoke. When properly broken the oxen should walk up when called. I guess we did not improve them, for we did not know much about bullocks. I know once Walter was driving them, and when he wanted them to stop he shouted out "Whoa!" and at the same time hit them with a big stick. Whether they were supposed to go on or to stop, would, I am sure, have puzzled wiser creatures than the oxen.

They were mostly used for ploughing, and mighty hard work it is, too, the first ploughing, or "breaking," as it is called; as of course the land that has been growing grass for centuries is one mass of roots, and the plough goes pop! pop! pop! cutting through them, sometimes coming to a dead stop at some extra thick bunch of roots. Every now and then the share has to be sharpened with a big file. It is very hard work for the animals, too, if they have much to do. For a small plough with a twelve-inch share, two oxen or three horses are generally used; but a good deal of breaking is done with a large plough of about twenty or twenty-four inch share, and from three to six yoke of oxen. Of course everybody does not own these things, and considerable business is done in breaking prairie by the acre.

After we had broken a considerable piece of land the various crops were put in. These consisted principally of Indian corn, spring wheat, oats, barley, potatoes, sorghum, or sugar cane, and a good number of different seeds in a patch of ground appropriated to garden uses. After this was all done fences had to be built to protect the crops from stray cattle and horses. Vast herds, belonging to people living miles away perhaps, wandered about at their own sweet will, and as we had very good spring water on our land it was rather a favourite pasture ground. Since that time, however, a herd law has been passed, so that no cattle are allowed to go about without a herder to keep them out of mischief during six months—viz., May to November. Fences are, therefore, no longer necessary, but still almost every one is trying to grow an osage-orange hedge. This is a prickly shrub that grows very rapidly, and bears a good deal of resemblance to an orange tree, including the fruit, though that is not edible.

We bought several head of cattle soon after settling, and as they were mostly cows with young calves, there was no difficulty in keeping them at home; all we had to do was to fasten the calves up. The oxen and horses when not at work were picketed out on the prairie by a long rope and a stake driven in the ground, until they were accustomed to the place. . . .

"Parker's Cellar"

Soon after the house was finished Parker set to work to dig a cellar in the side of a hill near by. I don't know exactly what he intended to make of it, but he commenced very enthusiastically, and soon made a bit of a show. Presently, though, he struck rock, and his progress was not so fast, and it really took him several weeks off and on before he got it to look much like a cellar. By this time the sun was scorching hot, and as he was working with nothing on his back but a thin shirt, and once not even that, his back became so burned that it was a mass of blisters, and for a fortnight he could do nothing. He never finished his undertaking, and ever since, although it has half fallen in, the big hole has been known as "Parker's Cellar."

I am afraid that we boys at first looked upon life on the prairie as being all fun and adventure, and could hardly see it in its right light; hence when we got some real work to do we were apt to shirk it, as being hardly what we had expected. Quite early in the spring after we had got some land broken, we were sent to plant about a bushel of haricot beans in one part of the field. We were not to plant a piece of land of any particular size, but to keep on planting until all the beans were used up. We started all right, putting in two or three beans every foot or so all along the furrow, but soon got tired of it, and so finding that we were using up the beans but slowly we began planting them a handful at a time. In this way we soon finished our task, but when the beans began to grow and came up a dozen times too thick, that let the cat out of the bag, and didn't we catch it hot then! We hadn't calculated on that.

Skunks

Upon first settling we were greatly troubled with skunks, which used to kill our fowls and steal our eggs. Our first acquaintance was made in this way. One day there was a great commotion among the chickens, and upon my looking under a small corn-crib to see what was the cause, a skunk snapped at my nose. Fortunately for me, though, he did not reach it, so I made for the house, and called Humphrey, who came and shot him with his revolver. Jack and I then dragged it out and skinned it, but the stench was so awful, that after having salted the pelt and nailed it to the side of the house, we could stand it no longer, and had to take it down and bury it. Those who have never seen, or rather smelled, a skunk can form no idea of the power of the perfume. . . .

Duck Keeping

Besides the noisy insects, the bull-frogs and the small frogs kept up a continual roar or croaking, so that music was not unknown on the prairie. The bull-frogs were tremendous creatures, measuring from nose to toes a foot to eighteen inches; their roar can he heard a mile or more. Fortunately they were not very numerous, but the small frogs were in every pond in myriads, but by degrees they got thinned out around us by our ducks. . . .

Besides all these things there were a good many wolves about us for some time, as our first attempts at duck-keeping well proved. Ducks are rather silly birds, and will not go into a house at night like hens, but prefer to take their repose either on the water or else on the banks. Hence they fall an easy prey to the coyotes, as the small prairie wolves are called. We bought a few ducks when we first moved up, and after losing most of them built a small sod house, and by careful attention managed to keep them for some time, driving them in every evening. But one night a stray pig broke the door down, and they were all carried away, save one old drake. We had the pleasure of seeing a wolf disappear over the hill in the morning, with the last duck on his shoulder. However, the pig kindly left us eighteen eggs, and by rare good luck we hatched them all under hens, and so got a good start again, much to the old drake's satisfaction. It was very amusing to see the fuss he made with the young ones.

Besides the coyotes, which we could hear barking almost every night, there were a few grey wolves in the neighbourhood, but both are getting scarce now, as they are hunted a good deal. An arrangement is made, that on a certain day all the young men for some miles around shall start from the outer edge of a large tract of country and ride towards an agreed centre, driving in any wolves they may come across. By the time all the horsemen are in sight of one another they may perhaps have six or eight wolves surrounded, which are then shot and killed.

The grey wolves are considered rather dangerous, but rarely attack a man unless in company, and goaded by hunger to desperation. The coyotes are arrant cowards.

Besides our ducks Jack had three geese, but was not very successful with them; for one was carried off by a wolf, the old gander was killed by a stray dog, and the other stupid old goose took to sitting, and there she "sot and sot" till she died—literally of starvation, despite all our efforts to make her feed. Thus ended Jack's speculation.

I was equally fortunate with my live stock. I had a little pig given me, and a very fine pig it grew; it was so long and so thin that we called it "the greyhound." It was a very intelligent animal though, and was a good one at a fence; in fact, it was impossible to keep it in a pen at all, and really became so knowing, that if upon finding it in the garden we called the dogs, it would immediately rush away and jump back into the pen before a dog had time to get it by the ear. After a while, when it had got pretty big, or rather long and tall, my father proposed to make pork of it, though more with the idea of getting rid of the mischievous thing than anything else, and so I traded him away, with a little to boot, for a heifer calf. The latter grew till she was two years old, and then laid down and died, and thus stopped my cattle-raising.

The Perils of a Young Mother on the Frontier

E.A. Van Court

In this memoir, Mrs. E.A. Van Court remembers her family's life in California between 1856 and 1864. During this period the Van Court's worked on a number of farms and ranches, mostly raising dairy cattle. Disease, floods, theft, and government dispossession led to failure in each venture. Van Court's writings show the mental and emotional stress that frontier life put on the settlers. She was overworked, isolated, and lonely. She had very little support especially during several childbirths. She had many fears and anxieties over bears, rattlesnakes, Indians, family illness and money—all with good reason. She even feared she was close to mental breakdown and suicide. Yet as she looked back on her life, a survivor at age eighty-two, she was proud of her accomplishments and at last "living a very comfortable, contented, peaceful life."

Early in August 1856, my husband became restless with City life and was determined to go out in the country and so went prospecting through Santa Clara Valley. Found a large ranch that took his fancy and leased one hundred and fifty acres for dairy purposes. The owner, a lawyer of some note in San Francisco, agreed to furnish us with one hundred cows, my husband to build a fence along the county road in front of the ranch, build a milk room, buy all necessary ar-

Excerpted from "Reminiscences," by Mrs. E.A. Van Court, *Western Americana Collection,* Beinecke Rare Book and Manuscript Library, Yale University.

ticles for the dairy, and share the profits with the owner. My husband went to work at daylight in the morning and kept at it till dark and kept his part of the contract to the letter; hired help to get the fences in order all around the ranch to be ready for the cows. As soon as the rainy season was on, one cow was furnished us and that was all we ever had. It soon became plain to us that we were to be cheated out of that lease. The owner had come across a man in poor health with money that took a fancy to the place, as it had a good house and it had a fine artesian well, and every thing in order, though he claimed that the cattle had gone up so high that he could not raise the money to buy them, which we knew was not so. We had no rent to pay, plenty of wood on that place and a nice lot of poultry and could make a living; and we were bound to stay till something was done for us.

Oldest Son Born

October 25th my oldest son was born, my first child having died in infancy before I came to California. This house was on a state road, the nearest neighbor a half a mile away, not a house in sight, very large old oak trees all through the Valley which gave the appearance of living in the forrest. I never lived on a ranch before, having been born and raised in a country village eighteen miles East of the City of Albany in New York State, and to be as I almost felt, in a foreign land, seven thousand miles from home among strangers in the condition I was. One can imagine my feelings day and night. Before I left San Francisco plans were made for a lady friend to come down and care for me. We were to send a note by the stage driver, he to give it to the lady's son-in-law at Wells Fargo's office in the City and she would come to us by return stage. My boy was born at three o'clock in the morning. The nearest neighbor came to me, brought a Spanish mid-wife with her who could not speak a word of English. I could not speak Spanish, but my neighbor could, and so we managed to get along. It was a very cold morning, the heaviest frost ever known in that Valley and it being the first night in five years my neighbor had been out, she caught a very severe cold walking through the wet grass, and I did not see her again in six weeks. She went home at seven in the morning. The Spanish woman left at ten, and from that hour on Saturday morning till the next Wednesday at two o'clock, my husband and I were alone in that house, not a soul in sight only as the stage passed eight o'clock in the morning. As was planned, my husband give the note to the stage driver on Sunday morning. The first note was given to the son-in-law and he jumped on his horse, rode quickly out to his home and started the lady on the stage, her baggage being sent the next day. It had seemed the very best way for news to reach her as we were ten miles from the Post Office, no telephones, no telegraphing, no cars, a day's travel to the City by stage. Only for the bravery of my husband and that Baby Boy, I think I would have lost my reason. My husband wanted to saddle the horse and go to Mayfield, try and find some one to come and help. I would have been left alone for two hours at least perhaps five and I would not consent. He insisted. I said "Just as sure as you go, I will get up and go out to the road." So together we fought it out. He caring for me as best he could, I caring for the baby. On Wednesday afternoon the stage stopped and the lady got off. I fell back on my pillow in a faint and never have had any recollection of seeing her enter the house. I came to and cried and cried till I was hysterical. I had surely reached the limit of my courage. I was in mortal fear of the Digger Indians and there were a plenty of them all through the Valley and treacherous people they are.

A Small Hotel

However, I was well cared for and in a couple of weeks was around the house and with the help of the kind lady was all right. She staid with me six weeks. Then one adversity after another followed us the nine long weary years in that Valley of St. Clara. We remained on that place until the next February when the owner of the Ranch became convinced that he could not get us off without some pay for all we had done, so had a talk with my husband and he said he would buy us a small hotel a half a mile down the road towards San Jose, give us the cow we had and six months rent. So we concluded to take the offer, and we left the ranch. . . .

My baby was only four months old when we took this place. I had no mother, sister or friend to even give me a thought and worked very hard from five o'clock in the morning till nine at night. From four to a dozen men stopping for meals any time of the day, had to make all my bread, pastry, no bakery for twelve miles; could not get help anywhere. I never had been alone on this place until after this family had left. They gave me a large Newfoundland dog, which I quickly made friends with, fed him well and he became very fond of me. After they had gone to Canada, I was very lonesome and suffered with fear day and night. It soon happened that groceries ran short which were very necessary to keep on hand. My husband said he would saddle the horse and go to Mountain View as fast as he could and get a supply. I said "Well, be sure and don't let the dog follow you." "I will look out for that," he said and so he started. I watched him out of sight. The dog did not follow him and I went about my work.

"We Do Not Sell Whiskey"

Soon after I heard a loud tramp in the bar room, went in to see what it was; there was an Indian with a long dirk knife sticking in a sheath outside of his pants, the handle and half of the blade in plain sight. He said to me, "Where is your hombre" meaning my husband. I instantly thought I must lie to save myself, and I told him, "He is behind the barn chopping wood." With that he knew I feared him and he began to jump up and down, swear at me in his own language and said, shaking his fist at me, "You give me whiskey." I told him I had no whiskey. He said, "You told me one damn big lie. Your hombre vamoose to Mountain View on the carriage; me savee." "We do not sell whiskey," I said. He called me a liar again. He was in a very savage mood. My baby was sitting on the floor in the parlor with pillows around him playing. I did not know what to do. I thought the dog had sneaked behind the trees and followed my husband and I nearly died right then. We did not sell liquor; my husband was greatly opposed to that, though the bar room was just as the family before us had left it, plenty of glasses and decanters on the shelves where I stood. I felt that I had to defend myself and the thought came to me that if he made an advance towards me, I could throw the decanters at him, but there was that dirk knife staring at me and I so very weak and trembly. The next thought was to come out from behind the counter, go to the baby and let the Indian have the house. I did so, I came out and when I got in the middle of the bar room, along the porch came the dog who had been asleep and heard the noise. He growled and came right up to my side. I was as brave then as if a dozen men had come to my rescue, only so weak I could hardly stand. I put my hand on the dogs head and petted him and I said to that Indian, "Now you vamoose, my dog eat you up." I knew the dog and I knew that the Indian would never have a chance to pull out that knife if I said "Seize him, Watch." And he evidently knew the dog, too, as he began to go out backwards swearing at me all the time, but made no attempt to pull out that knife.

I just staggered to the porch, sat down on the bench the dog by my side, and I am sure for ten minutes I could not have gone into the parlor and picked up that baby. My husband after being gone two hours, thought I had a sick headache. I was in such a plight and that experience unnerved me for a long time; that the last time I was ever all alone on that place. We both worked very hard, raised a large lot of chickens which brought us a good income and after we had been there about five months, a disease came among them and in ten days we lost every one, two hundred and ten in number. The disease (I have forgotten the name) was from an accumulation of fat all through the body and as soon as the fat covered the heart they dropped dead. I assure you we were very discouraged.

I could not stand the hard work any longer and was breaking down, and as our six months free rent was nearly up, we made up our minds to leave. We knew not where. One afternoon a man drove up to the door for dinner and also wanted some tools of some kind to mend his harness which was broken, and he sat there on the porch about an hour talking to my husband and in the course of the conversation, he said he was looking for a good dairyman. He had sixty-five cows and milked all the time thirty of them. He made us a very good offer, so we picked up and left the place.

We soon got on our feet again, though I did not regain my strength and in six months I went down flat with nervous prostration. I could not sleep, I could not eat and all looked dark for me, and my husband also, as the Doctor told my husband that I was going into a decline. So help had to be gotten to do what I had been doing. I could not walk a dozen steps from the house. We were lucky enough to get the same lady from San Francisco who had attended me at the birth of my boy and she staid with us through the winter; took good care of me and I rallied again and late in the next fall when every cow on the ranch got sick sores all over their bags and their eyes, it was impossible to milk them any longer. This was caused from the alkali near the Bay. Many of the cows died and it was a great loss to the owner and there were no profits to share with us any longer, and we had to give up. There was nothing else for us to do.

It was late in the season, the rains coming and the only thing that offered was to go up to Mountain View, rent a house there while something else offered. My husband worked at his trade through the winter; while there my little boy took sick with lung fever. No Doctor was nearer than San Jose, twelve miles away and they would not come. The wind was terrible; there was nothing to do but take good care of him with the remedies of our grandmothers' days and after two weeks, he recovered, and I thank God he lives today.

Dispossessed

My husband took a small place the next spring and raised a patch of potatoes and the next fall bought a ranch of thirty acres, kept a cow, raised another fine lot of chickens and put in a crop of hay and barley; had good luck and made a payment on the ranch. My youngest son was born there, September 21, 1860.

After two years there we made the last payment in August and we were dispossessed by the United States Government. Our land was included in the nine leagues of land given to Castro, being the first ranch lying between New Mountain View and the Bay. This was one of the famous Mexican grants. We had the same as all others on the claim, a squatter's title, but it was not considered. . . . Many a man would have committed suicide had they been in my husband's place, but he was of better material than that. He was game through it all. His family was all the world to him and he would not be downed, so went prospecting through the San Mateo Mountains, Coast Range to within three miles of Pescadero, leased five hundred acres of land. The owner to put on one hundred cows for dairying, make butter and cheese, share the profits with him. My husband came to San Francisco after his family. He had moved our belongings while I was away. The early part of November, we went from Mayfield to the ranch in a buggy started early in the morning. We were well supplied with lunch for the day and milk for the baby; fourteen months old, and after passing the foot hills, we rested, staked the horse out for feed and ate our lunch. Then we started across the mountains to the ranch, which was a half mile to the Ocean. It was very dark when we reached the worst place, called Bear Gulch, where we got down at the bottom of the Gulch. . . .

Bears, Floods, Coyotes

There were real live bears all through those mountains and the road was right through this Gulch. When we reached the top of that mountain, we could see the light in the house of the owner of the ranch we were to take. We reached that house at nine o'clock where we were kindly treated, stayed three days, then went to the other house we were to live in. We had a fine lot of chickens, one horse, buggy, twelve pigs and our household goods. In less than a month on Christmas morning, the great flood of '61 and '62 began. We were too far up the mountain for our house to be carried off, but in one month everything we had was gone, but the buggy and chickens and household goods. Our old family horse we found one morning dead at our kitchen door. The bears came down the ravine near the house and ate up our pigs. The chickens were safe in a good hen house. Cattle all around the mountains perished, what were left could not be milked, they were living skeletons. We managed to keep the cow, so as we had in the barn barley and some hay brought from our old home, when they moved our live stock. The rain was on for five weeks, just pouring torrents; the valleys were ankle deep with water and the mountain slides terrible; during that dark and awful month we got out of light and had none for three weeks, only three miles from stores in Pescadero, but it was impossible to cross that San Gregaria Creek. You can imagine what must have been the feeling of a mother with two little ones, liable to get sick in any of those dark and terrible nights. Coyotes coming down the mountains in droves, barking like hungry wolves, cattle bellowing and rubbing up against the house for shelter, the ocean roaring like mad. . . .

Back to Santa Clara Valley

In February, it began to clear up and the weather was fine. The owner of all this land could not buy the cows as he expected and promised. He was honest enough and very kind to us; all the stock he had, less than a dozen perished, he could do nothing. He had to give up the 500 extra acres he had yet unpaid for only a small homestead left. There was certainly nothing left for us to do but get out of those mountains and go back to Santa Clara Valley and try our luck, but it was impossible to leave then as the roads were all broken up. So we worried along till the middle of May when my last child was born. No nurse, the nearest Doctor twenty miles away. When this child was born there was a lady with me through the night. The morning she was four days old I got up at seven o'clock, began to pack our belongings. The morning she was ten days old, we started out. The fog so thick we could not see the mountains so very near us. Five of us were seated in the buggy and rode sixty-five miles to the home of a friend near Saratoga. On going over the ridge to Half Moon Bay, twelve miles we had to get out of the buggy. My husband tied the wheels to keep it from pitching down the banks. I carried the baby in one arm leading the boy baby, twenty months old by the hand and the five years old boy trotting by the side of his father who lead the horse. We all got into the buggy when we came to hard ground and many a steep place we crossed before we got to Half Moon Bay on the main road. We stopped at a farm house, the lady of the house making me a cup of tea and urging us to stay with her a couple of days. She thought it terrible for me to be travelling over the rough roads with three little children, the youngest only ten days old. But the fog had all gone the day was warm and bright and I more than anxious to get out of the mountains and reach our destination. Which we did that night at dark.

Hoodoo Was Over Us

The friends we stopped with let us have an empty house they had on the ranch close to the one they lived in and as soon as our household goods came in three days after, we settled there for the summer. My husband worked hard at harvesting. My baby took sick with marasmus, a disease that drys the body up with fever and was sick all summer, very sick, until we were induced to try homeopathy and she was cured in three weeks, weighed eight pounds when born and exactly the same at four months old. . . .

In September we moved from there, took a ranch on shares, ploughed the ground and put in a crop of wheat and the dryest season known in that valley followed the winters flood and the hot sun burned everything all up and we did not raise a pound of wheat. On this place we had no water, had to go two miles to Campbell's Creek once a week; the men folks would take a large lumber wagon holding six barrels and go after the water. For my part, I was really and truly discouraged and the country was no place for us and a hoodoo was over us. . . . As our oldest boy was then seven years old and must go to school and so we decided to go back to San Francisco. After nine years of hard struggles and privations all we had to take with us was one cow giving a fine mess of milk. We thought with the three young children we could not leave the cow behind; we sold our chickens, one horse and buggy. My husband had been down to the City and secured a house for us on the corner of Laguna and Hayes Street near good friends and with the house was a large back yard, well fenced and in that we put the cow. We had all the milk we wanted and sold enough to pay our rent, $18.00 a month. We got started; my husband had a good position in a shoe house and all seemed bright when we had been there less than a month, I opened my back door to go out for water and that gate was open, the cow gone and from that day to this, we never hear of that cow. My husband spent three days down the road to hunt for the cow: no trace of her did we get. We wrote to our neighbors where we had left; no one had seen her. We surely thought that the ill luck would follow us wherever we went.

Success in Oakland

There was nothing left for us to do but face the music, go on, let come what would, do the best we could. So we stayed in the City until all our children were out of school, eighteen years. Then we came to Oakland March 4th, 1882. My husband worked in a mill. I began taking boarders which I made a success of (twenty-four in number), on Harrison Street between 14th and 19th, sold out April 15th, 1912 at the age of 80 years and four months, and I will say here that many women that I knew in early days crossing the plains in '49–50 and '52 suffered more than I, yet the most of them had been raised on the frontier when many states were unsettled and they were used to hardships which the Eastern women knew nothing of, the settling up of new countries and that made it harder to endure. It was here on Harrison Street that my husband died at the age of 72 surrounded by his family and in comfort. He passed away at one o'clock on the 25th day of October, 1888.

This is the true story of my pioneer life in California and I am more than 82 years and three months old, living a very comfortable, contented, peaceful life, happy with the love of my children and many good, kind and loving friends. I hope the reading of it by the young people of the State that are surrounded with every luxury and convenience denied their parents will realize how very blessed they are. I thank God for my life, my health and beautiful Oakland, where I hope to spend my last days. Whenever the call comes I will be able to say, "My work is done, I am content."

Sod Busting in Nebraska

Rolf Johnson

Rolf Johnson was nineteen in 1876 when he began writing his
diary. That year he moved with his parents from Illinois to
Phelps County, Nebraska. Rolf's parents were from southern
Sweden and came to the United States in 1854. They were
part of a great swell of almost ten thousand people who left
Sweden because of bad economic conditions and religious
oppression in the 1850s. They settled in Illinois but when the
great drought of 1873 hit they moved to Nebraska. Due to the
Homestead Act, the Johnsons could file a claim with ten dollars and get 160 acres of government land. All they had to do
was "prove up"—live on it for five years and make certain
improvements. Rolf Johnson's diary gives a lively depiction
of what it was like for a family to make good their claim.
Rolf's earlier diary entries while living in Illinois were
mostly about going to parties and kissing girls, but when he
moved to Nebraska his writing details a harder life: building
sod houses, plowing the prairie, digging wells, and hunting.
However, he did manage to find the time to take girls ox-
riding. Rolf's diary also shows how the pioneer community
helped one another survive the difficult conditions of farming
and living on the frontier.

M arch 11
   This morning we started for "Phelps Center" (as the
site of the new colony is called) with four loads of lumber.

Excerpted from *Happy as a Big Sunflower: Adventures in the West, 1876–1880*, by Rolf
Johnson, edited by Richard E. Jensen (Lincoln: University of Nebraska Press, with the
Nebraska State Historical Society, 2000).

Besides Dahlstrom and I there were two loads of lumber for the erection of an emigrant house in Phelps Center, by Rylander and Hallgren. These teams were driven by Frank Hallgren and Charley Nelson.

After crossing the Platte we turned west and drove up the valley some twenty miles when we came to Williamsburg, the county seat of Phelps Co., containing 4 houses, a school house, courthouse (an unpretentious frame building) and two dwelling houses. One of the latter, belonging to A.S. Baldwin, has been opened as a temporary hotel by a Dane named Albert Hansen and his wife, and here we put up for the night. . . .

March 12

This morning we drove out some seven or eight miles south to where Dahlstrom had two carpenters at work building a house. We found them living in the cellar, over part of which they had made a roof, and fixed a fireplace in the wall and when we came up [they] were cooking coffee and graham bread. They invited us to "pitch in" for our dinner which we did.

As far as the eye could reach in any direction, not a sign of human habitation was visible (except about 3 miles south east where Rylander and Hallgren are building an emigrant house and digging a well for the accommodation of the colonists). Nothing but miles and miles of level prairie burnt black by the prairie fire. Hundreds of thousands of bleaching buffalo skeletons are scattered over the plains showing what a terrible slaughter of these animals has been going. In Kearney I saw mountains of buffalo bones along the railroad track, where they had been hauled for shipment east.

Dahlstrom and I unloaded our wagons and went back to Williamsburg, where we found Leander Hallgren with a party of land hunters from the east.

This evening most of the party have been playing dominos, while I have been reading a Danish book I borrowed of Mrs. Hansen.

March 13

Weather mild and pleasant. Drove in to Kearney this

forenoon. A large outfit of men, wagons, and mules from St. Joe, Mo. under the leadership of Tom Davis, bound for the Black Hills, camped here to day. They are well armed and do not fear the Indians. I spent a portion of the afternoon in their camp.

Father has bought a yoke of oxen and a wagon of Mr. Brant for one hundred and twenty five dollars.

March 14

This morning a long caravan of wagons drawn by horses, mules, and oxen, and loaded with household utensils and farming implements pulled out of Kearney, crossed the river and wended its way westward. It was the emigrants, the "pioneers of the plains," going out to found a Swedish settlement in Phelps County. The women and children were packed like sardines in one wagon and hurried on ahead. The weather was intensely cold and I had to walk to keep warm. I drove our oxen, a pair of wild, half-broken Texas steers called Jerry and Bryan. I had a big load and a small team not much used to steady pulling, so I was the last one to reach Williamsburg, where I arrived about 9 o'clock P.M.

The oxen got so tired at last they actually laid down every hundred yards or so and it took me about 2 hours to drive the last mile. Father drove one of Dahlstrom's teams so he was ahead.

When I got to Williamsburg I found the emigrants crowded into John Shafer's little house, which he had kindly opened to them.

Sleeping on the Hotel Floor

March 15

Last night over 30 persons slept on the floor in Shafer's house. This morning the weather being very cold it was concluded to have the women and children at Williamsburg until the weather moderates. Most of the men went on to Phelps Center with the loaded wagons. Mr. & Mrs. A.P. Anderson and our family moved into the hotel, where we are comparatively comfortable. I have passed the time reading one of Baldwin's books, "The Gold Hunters in Europe or The Dead Alive" by W.W. Thomes. Charley Nelson's already large family was further increased by the arrival to day of a little "bug eater," name at present unknown. He was born in Shafer's house and is the first child of Swede descent born in Phelps County.

A blinding storm of wind and snow is raging this afternoon so it is impossible to see 100 feet.

March 16

Slept on the floor of the hotel last night and was so cold I could not sleep. Cold but not stormy weather. . . .

"Dugouts"

April 9

Father and sister Hilda attended the funeral of Mrs. Hakanson, an old lady who died in Williamsburg a couple of days ago of consumption. She was the mother of Aug. Carlson and was buried on his claim about 2 miles north of here.

April 12

I have had the toothache without intermission for 24 hours. It nearly drives me crazy.

April 14

Stenfelt and I went down to Williamsburg and bought a load of hay of old Jim Steward. Stopped there to dinner and had fricasseed grouse. Hay is worth $4 per ton.

April 15

Father and I have been down to Spring Creek after a load of elm poles, which we brought of old Sam Moser for $1.50.

Spring Creek, in the south western corner of this county, is different from all other creeks I have ever seen being nothing more or less than a deep canyon with precipitous wall[s] filled with trees in the midst of which flows a small stream which empties into the Republican river, some 15 miles below. It is settled nearly its entire length, the settlers mostly living in "dugouts" which is partly a cave and partly built of logs and mud. They are perched here and there on the steep banks and hidden away in crevices like so many swallows nests. . . .

Building Sod Houses

April 17

Finished Dahlstrom's well so now we have an abundance of cold, clear water. It is 110 feet deep.

We are very busy these days building sod houses and stables and hauling hay for the stock and material for building.

April 20

Father went down to Turkey Creek yesterday and got back to day. He bought a cow, a sow, a dozen of hens, and

Prairie Marriage

Jessie Rowland was the daughter of a Kansas justice of the peace. She often went with her father as he performed marriage ceremonies. She describes one such pioneer wedding in 1870. It took place in the bride's family home—a one room dugout with two chairs and a dirt floor. Afterward, the wedding supper was laid out and Rowland's father was paid. And then for the newlyweds, as Rowland says in her remembrance, "came the test of trying to live happily ever after."

My father, being one of the early pioneers and a justice of the peace, was called upon many times to report "Wilt thou, Mary?" and "Wilt thou, John?" Then came the test of trying to live happily ever after.

On one of those occasions my father was asked to preside at a wedding ten miles away from our home and my mother received an invitation to accompany him. Upon arriving at their destination they were ushered down six steps into a dugout, where the mother of the bride was preparing a wedding feast. There was but one room and the furniture consisted of two chairs, one with only two rounds to the back and bottoms. A bed made of scantlings, a board table, a short bench, a stove, and a motto hung over the door, "God Bless Our Home."

There was no floor, and a sheet had been stretched across one corner of the room. The bride and groom were stationed behind this, evidently under the impression it would not be proper to appear until time for the ceremony, but they were some corn costing in all sixty-seven dollars.

April 21

J.P. Landquist, who boards at Dahlstrom's, helped father and I put a roof on our house to day.

April 25

Saw four antelopes.

Removed from Dahlstrom's cellar to our new house, which is about a quarter of a mile from Dahlstrom's. I will attempt to describe how it was built:

---

in such close quarters and the sheet was so short it put one in mind of an ostrich when it tries to hide by sticking its head in the sand.

Mrs. Brown, we will call her, was grinding something in a coffee mill but arose to receive her guests with all the dignity of the first lady of the land. She placed one chair for my mother and one for my father; seating herself upon the bench, she continued turning the coffee grinder. Soon after some of the neighbors came in, and at the appointed time the bride and groom emerged arm in arm from behind the temporary curtain and, stepping forward to where my father was sitting, all became quiet and he pronounced the words that made them one.

Soon after all sat down to the wedding supper. The sheet that hung across the corner of the room was taken down and spread over the table for a cloth. Mrs. Brown's efforts at the coffee mill had turned out some delicious coffee, made of dried carrots. There were seven different kinds of sauce, all made out of wild plums put up in seven different ways. The rest of the menu was quite simple and consisted of plain bread and butter, and fried pork. The table was shoved close to the bed and three sat on that side while three sat on the bench. The chairs were occupied and two or three kegs finished out the number of seats.

After supper the bridegroom took my father to one side and asked him to accept some potatoes in payment for performing the ceremony. He readily accepted and returned home.

Joanna Stratton, *Pioneer Women: Voices from the Kansas Frontier.* New York: Simon and Schuster, 1981.

First we broke sod with a breaking plow; this we cut off into bricks which were 2 feet long, 12 inches wide and four inches thick; of this we built the walls of the house. In the center of the house is a big crotch; in this and on the end walls rests the ridge pole; next come the rafters, about 1 1/2 feet apart, which are simply round poles of elm, ash, and cottonwood with the bark on. On top of this is a layer of willows; on top of them a thin layer of sod and over all about six inches of dirt. We have a cellar and board floor though it is something unusual in a sod house.

The house is 16×21 feet inside and the walls are two feet thick. Its gables stand north and south. On the west side is a door and half a window, on the east a half window and on the south a whole window. These houses are very comfortable being cool in summer and warm in winter. . . .

Run Over

April 29

Went down to the Platte after a load of wood. When I got back and was trying to unhitch the ox chain the oxen started to run away. I was knocked down, run over, and kicked by the oxen and run over by the wagon too. Fortunately I was not much hurt, though mother came running pale as death thinking I would be killed.

Sun. April 30

I am sore all over to day and the imprint of Jerry's hoofs are to be seen on several parts of my body.

May 3

Went down to the Platte after a load of wood. Stopped at Williamsburg to get my mail. The post master is William A. Dilworth, Clerk of Phelps Co., and son of Old Gen. Dilworth.

Sun. May 7

Had a snow storm yesterday, snow all thawed off to day. This evening while I was writing a letter to Uncle Lewis, mother started to go out, and as she opened the door she encountered an antelope on the threshold. Before I could get my gun he was gone. I guess the light streaming through the window attracted it. Antelope are pretty numerous and we see them every day. They are of the variety called "pronghorns."

May 9

I have been with Frank and Leander Hallgren out in the western part of the county surveying. We drove in a buggy and had a fine ride over the plains. While eating lunch at noon an antelope trotted up to within 100 yards of us and stopped. Frank fired at it and missed and it trotted off. . . .

Breaking Prairie

May 12

Had a splendid time trying to break prairie with our oxen!

They were unaccustomed to pulling a plow and tried to walk in forty directions at once. Several times they made a beeline for the stable and then there was music by the whole band and we would waltz out on the prairie again.

Sun. May 21

Emil, Justus, and I started to explore a range of sandhills 4 or 5 miles north east of here. We had a pleasant walk over the prairie, which is carpeted with a soft velvety coat of buffalo grass and many varieties of prairie flowers.

From the top of one of the hills we had a fine view of the surrounding country. To the east stretched a thousand hills clothed with green grass; to the north the broad valley of the Platte, with the river like a belt of silver with its emerald isles; to the south and west the vast plain with the settlement lay stretched out like a map before us. We found a relic of prehistoric times on this hill. It was an arrowhead of flint.

May 23

Big storm of wind and rain yesterday and Dahlstrom's, Anderson's and our cattle stampeded. We have been hunting them to day horseback. Couldn't find them. This evening at dusk as I was returning to Dahlstrom's I rode under the clothes line and nearly sawed my head off.

Dahlstrom, Aleck Danielson, J. Anderson, and my father, who were out hunting cattle, did not return this evening.

May 24

The cow hunters came home to day with the cattle. They

struck the trail yesterday in a draw east of here, followed it over the sandhills and found the cattle a[t] George Bleakman's on the Platte nine miles away. They stopped at Bleakman's over night.

An antelope came up within 25 yards of the children who were out in the field. Our dog Terry sprang at it and caught it by the leg. The antelope kicked the dog on the nose, made him let go, and lit out for the sandhills.

May 27

Slew my first rattlesnake with an axe about 40 rods from the house. He was over three feet long and sported seven rattles.

Sun. May 28

We had a number of visitors: Salgren & family; Dahlstrom and family; Mr. & Mrs. J. Anderson, Charley Johnson, and Aleck Danielson.

May 30

Father, Dahlstrom, and I have been over to Johannes Anderson's to help him break his oxen to the plow.

Father is now working for Dahlstrom at $20 per month while I stay at home, break prairie, plant corn & c.

June 3

As Emil and I were returning from a trip to the Platte we saw a large hawk sitting on the prairie. We drove toward it and just as it rose to fly I fired and brought it down with a broken wing. I then dismounted and secured it, though not without a struggle in which I was both clawed and bitten. We brought it home and tied it up to a stake.

June 6

Killed my hawk to day. He was so savage he attacked every one who went near him.

Saw a herd of six antelopes grazing between our house and Dahlstroms.

June 8

Attended a breaking bee at Chas. Nelson's. There were 10 teams and we broke up ten acres.

Sadly in want of rain. The ground is so dry and hard it is almost impossible to plow. . . .

New Settlers Every Week

June 21

Johannes Anderson, Aleck Danielson, Aaron W. Johnson, Andrew Olson, and I have been down on Spring Creek after wood. After driving a mile or so on the way back the tire came off one of the hind wheels of my wagon and all the felloes crushed so I had to throw off my load and go home without it. It was late this evening and it was so dark, we had great difficulty in finding our way home.

John P. Bragg of Oneida, Ills. is staying with us. He is out looking at the country with a view to locate. New settlers are coming out every week and our settlement has more than doubled since last spring.

June 23

We have no well so we have a big barrel and a sled and every day I haul a barrel of water from Dahlstrom's.

Made the acquaintance of Clarence Peterson, a young hunter from Harlan Co. He was out hunting to day and shot two antelope, which he divided among the settlers.

Kearney, Neb. June 26

Went into Kearney to get the wheel repaired that was broken on the trip from Spring Creek. I am stopping at Brandt's.

June 29

Got back from Kearney. Wilma Carlson, daughter of August Carlson rode with me out. First time I ever took a girl ox-riding.

July 4

I celebrated the [nation's] centennial by sowing and harrowing three acres of buckwheat.

Chronology

1775

March 16: Daniel Boone sets out to blaze the Wilderness Road from the Cumberland Gap to Kentucky.

April 1: Boone founds Boonesborough in Kentucky.

April 18: The American Revolution starts with the first shots fired at Lexington and Concord, Massachusetts.

1783

The Revolutionary War ends. Britain and the United States sign a peace treaty that gives the United States all territory east of the Mississippi River.

1803

President Thomas Jefferson purchases Louisiana from France for $15 million, doubling the size of the United States.

1804

The Lewis and Clark Expedition leaves from St. Louis on May 14.

1805

Lewis and Clark reach the Pacific Ocean in the present-day state of Oregon.

1810

The population of the United States is 7.2 million, an increase of over 36 percent since 1800.

1815

The United States defeats the British in the last battle of the War of 1812.

1821

William Becknell, a trader, leads a trading party to Santa Fe in the present-day state of New Mexico, mapping the Santa Fe Trail.

1824

Fur trader James Bridger discovers the Great Salt Lake in Utah. Jedediah Smith, a guide for the Rocky Mountain Fur Company, leads a trading expedition through the South Pass of the Rocky Mountains that will be a key pass to California.

1830

April 10: William L. Sublette leads ten wagons out of St. Louis, Missouri, over what would become known as the Oregon Trail.

May 28: President Andrew Jackson signs the Indian Removal Act, which begins the policy of removing the eastern Indian tribes to lands west of the Mississippi River.

July 15: The Fox, Sauk, and Sioux tribes sign a treaty that gives the United States most of the land in the present-day states of Iowa, Minnesota, and Missouri.

1832

Hall Jackson Kelley and Nathaniel J. Wyeth guide separate expeditions of wagon trains to Oregon.

1839

Cherokee, Choctaw, Chickasaw, Creek, and Seminoles are forced to march from their lands in the southern states to the reservation in Oklahoma during what was known as the Trail of Tears. Thousands of Indians die on this journey.

August: John Sutter, a Swiss emigrant trader, arrives in the Sacramento valley to become one of the first white settlers in that region.

1841

The first large wagon train of pioneers reaches California traveling over the Oregon Trail.

1842

Colonel John C. Frémont explores and maps the Oregon Trail.

1843

James Bridger opens Fort Bridger on the Green River in southwest Wyoming. It becomes an important supply and rest stop on the Oregon Trail.

May 22: One thousand settlers set out from Elm Grove, Missouri, in a wagon train bound for Oregon.

1844

Joseph Smith, the leader of the Mormons, is killed by a mob after being jailed in Carthage, Illinois. Brigham Young succeeds Smith as the leader of the Mormon Church.

December 4: James Polk is elected president. Polk is in favor of acquiring Texas, California, and Oregon as U.S. territories.

1845

Frémont publishes his journals and maps of his expeditions in the Rocky Mountains and along the Oregon Trail, which will become guides for a generation of pioneers moving west.

December 29: Texas becomes the twenty-eighth state of the Union.

1846

February 10: Mormons begin their exodus from Illinois led by Brigham Young.

May 13: After Mexican forces attack U.S. soldiers in Texas, Congress declares war on Mexico.

June 15: The U.S. Senate approves a treaty with Great Britain giving Oregon to the United States and establishing the U.S.-British boundary at the forty-ninth parallel.

November: The Donner party is snowbound in the California Sierra Nevada. Of the original eighty-nine that left Independence, Missouri, in July, only forty-five survive.

1847
Young and his Mormons arrive at their new home in Great Salt Lake Basin on April 16.

1848
January 24: Gold is discovered at Sutter's Creek, located on the American River in California's Sacramento valley.

February 2: The United States and Mexico sign the Treaty of Guadalupe Hidalgo, ending the Mexican-American War. The United States gains the territories of New Mexico, Nevada, Utah, Colorado, and California.

November 7: Zachary Taylor, who had led the U.S. forces to victory in Mexico, is elected president.

1850
August 13: California becomes the thirty-first state; slavery is prohibited in the state.

September 26: Young is appointed governor of the Utah Territory.

1853
On March 2, Congress organizes the Washington Territory, making the forty-sixth parallel the boundary between Oregon and Washington.

1855
The U.S. Army defeats the Ute and Jacarilla Apache, making travel along the Santa Fe Trail safe for settlers and traders.

1856

The first company of Mormon "handcart pioneers" leaves Iowa City for Salt Lake City on June 9.

1859

On February 14, Oregon becomes the thirty-third state; it is admitted to the Union as a free state.

1860

Abraham Lincoln is elected president.

1861

Civil War begins as Confederate batteries bombard Fort Sumter.

1862

President Lincoln signs the Homestead Act on May 20. This law provides that any citizen who is the head of a family can claim 160 acres of public land after living on it for five years.

1864

On November 29, Colorado volunteers attack the Cheyenne village at Sand Creek and massacre 450 Indians, including many women and children.

1865

January: Cheyenne, Arapaho, and Sioux warriors launch revenge attacks against settlers along the Platte River in Colorado.

April 9: Robert E. Lee surrenders to Ulysses S. Grant, ending the Civil War.

1868

April 29: The Sioux and Cheyenne agree to live on reservations in the Dakota Territory.

July 28: The Fourteenth Amendment is ratified. It gives full rights and citizenship to African Americans and to all others born or naturalized in the United States. Native Americans are denied citizenship.

1869

May 10: The first transcontinental railroad is completed.

December 10: Women are granted the right to vote and to hold office in the territory of Wyoming, the first state or territory to grant this right to women.

1873

Congress passes the Timber Culture Act on March 3. This law allows settlers to claim 160 acres of government land in return for planting forty acres of trees.

1874

Grasshopper plagues destroy crops on the prairies from Texas to Canada. Thousands of settlers return east.

1876

The Battle of the Little Bighorn occurs on June 25. Lieutenant Colonel George Custer and his entire command are killed by a large force of Indian warriors from various tribes.

1878

Farmers flock to the Dakotas during the Great Dakota Boom. Settlers claim 1.4 million acres in homestead grants.

1889

Oklahoma is opened up for white settlement on April 22. Thousands of settlers stake their claims on land formerly belonging to Seminole and Creek Indians.

1890

The U.S. Census Bureau announces the closing of the frontier.

For Further Research

Stephen Ambrose and Douglas Brinkley, eds., *Witness to America*. New York: HarperCollins, 1999.

John Bakeless, ed., *The Journals of Lewis and Clark*. New York: Penguin Books USA, 1964.

T.D. Bonner, ed., *The Life and Adventures of James P. Beckwourth*. New York: Knopf, 1931.

Edwin Bryant, *What I Saw in California*. Lincoln: University of Nebraska Press, 1985.

Percy G. Ebbutt, *Emigrant Life in Kansas*. London: Swan Sonnenschein, 1886.

John Filson, *The Discovery and Settlement of Kentucke*. Ann Arbor, MI: University Microfilms, 1966.

John E. Findling, ed., *Events That Changed America in the Nineteenth Century*. Westport, CT: Greenwood, 1997.

Timothy Flint, *Recollections of the Last Ten Years*. Carbondale: Southern Illinois University Press, 1968.

Joseph Lewis French, *The Pioneer West*. Boston: Little, Brown, 1923.

Leroy R. Hafen, *Handcarts to Zion*. Glendale, CA: Arthur H. Clark, 1960.

Lansford W. Hastings, *The Emigrants' Guide to Oregon and California*. Princeton, NJ: Princeton University Press, 1932.

Kenneth L. Holmes, ed., *Covered Wagon Women: Diaries and Letters from the Western Trails, 1840–1849*. Lincoln: University of Nebraska Press, 1995.

Paul Johnson, *A History of the American People*. New York: HarperCollins, 1998.

Rolf Johnson, *Happy as a Big Sunflower: Adventures in the West, 1876–1880.* Lincoln: University of Nebraska Press, 2000.

Phoebe Goodell Judson, *A Pioneer's Search for an Ideal Home.* Lincoln: University of Nebraska Press, 1984.

William Loren Katz, *The Black West.* Seattle: Open Hand, 1987.

Fanny Kelly, *Narrative of My Captivity Among the Sioux Indians.* Chicago: R.R. Donnelley & Sons, 1990.

Gerda Lerner, ed., *Women's Diaries of the Westward Journey.* New York: Schocken Books, 1982.

Fred Lockley, *Conversations with Pioneer Women.* Eugene, OR: Rainy Day, 1981.

Randolph B. Marcy, *The Prairie Traveler.* New York: Harper and Brothers, 1859.

James Knox Polk Miller, *The Road to Virginia City.* Norman: University of Oklahoma Press, 1960.

Ruth B. Moynihan, ed., *So Much to Be Done.* Lincoln: University of Nebraska Press, 1990.

Virginia Reed Murphy, *Across the Plains in the Donner Party.* Silverthorne, CO: Vistabooks, 1995.

Robert E. Riegel, ed., *America Moves West.* New York: Holt, Rinehart, and Winston, 1964.

Sarah Royce, *A Frontier Lady: Recollections of the Gold Rush and Early California.* New Haven, CT: Yale University Press, 1932.

Sanford Wexler, *Westward Expansion: An Eyewitness History.* New York: Facts On File, 1991.

Index